Curious Cargo

Also by Patrick Semple

A Parish Adult Education Handbook – Editor

Believe It Or Not – A Memoir

That Could Never Be – with K Dalton

The Rectory Dog – Poetry Collection

The Rector Who Wouldn't Pray For Rain – A Memoir

A Narrow Escape – Poetry Collection

Transient Beings – A Novel

CURIOUS CARGO

Patrick Semple

**Voyages to
The West Indies, South and Central America
and the Mediterranean.**

Code Green Publishing

ISBN 978-1-907215-20-9

Version 1.0

Cover design by Code Green Publishing

ACKNOWLEDGEMENTS

I would like to thank our fellow passengers on the Caribbean voyage who contributed so much to our enjoyment of that adventure, the crews on both voyages and the representatives of Horn and Grimaldi shipping lines.

Names have been changed to protect anonymity.

I want to thank Brendan Kennelly for permission to quote from his poem 'The Good'.

For Tegan and Naiya

THE WEST INDIES, SOUTH
AND CENTRAL AMERICA

First Voyage: Dover, Antwerp, Le Havre, through the Azores (without stopping), straight across the Atlantic to West Indies, Pointe-à-Pitre (Guadeloupe), Fort-de-France (Martinique), Turbo (Colombia), Moin (Costa Rica) then straight back to Ponta Delgada (The Azores).

CHAPTER 1

Two thirds of the surface of the earth is covered in water. From time immemorial man has crossed the seas of the world to explore, to trade and to prosecute war. The first boats were dugouts, hollowed out tree trunks, powered by men with paddles and oars. Then sailors learned to harness the sea's temperamental partner, wind, to travel faster and with less effort. Man will always find ways to do things with less effort. This method culminated in the great sailing ships that were used by the early adventurers who explored the globe. In the nineteenth century steam superseded sail which was in turn superseded by the internal combustion engine that gave us the great passenger liners of the twentieth century and the giant container ships, tankers and bulk carriers of today.

There is something special about being at sea. To stand on the deck of a ship in a vast expanse of ocean on a starry night looking at the unfathomable immensity of the heavens is, even for the most unreflective person, to pose questions about the universe, meaning and life itself. Since the advent of air travel there are many young travellers who have never experienced the sensations of being at sea. They haven't even crossed the Irish Sea by ship when land is out of sight for only a short time. No longer do passengers sail into the Mediterranean on the way to the East or cross the Atlantic on great liners. My wife, Hilary, and I crossed from New York to Cobh in June 1971 on *Niewe Amsterdam*, one of those great liners. Later that year *Niewe Amsterdam* made her last scheduled crossing of the Atlantic. Cruise ships have become a familiar part of the tourist industry. These ships spend a day or two at sea and then disgorge their well-heeled passengers at fashionable ports to spend a day sightseeing and to retreat again to the luxury of their floating hotel. This kind of voyaging gives little insight into the realities of life at sea in contrast to the way that travelling as one of a handful of passengers on a working cargo vessel does.

Navigating the high seas carries risks. An unsound or carelessly handled ship can spell disaster; wind and sea are unforgiving. It is said that few sailors can swim, so they rely entirely on safety systems; these days, life-jackets, lifeboats and satellite contact ashore and with other ships.

Recently Hilary and I went on a voyage on a cargo ship carrying eleven passengers to the West Indies and Central and South America. When we planned the voyage however we didn't bargain on having to make for our muster station in the middle of the Atlantic to await orders to take to the boats to abandon ship.

When I hear the song 'The White Cliffs of Dover' it brings me back to early mornings in the communal bathroom of the student hostel I lived in over 40 years ago. Davey, a fellow student, now a Franciscan friar, would make his entrance singing at the top of his voice 'The White Cliffs of Dover', the song that Vera Lynn, the British Forces' sweetheart, made famous during World War II.

His purpose, of course, was to provoke a response from whoever was already in the bathroom, most of whom were still half asleep struggling to come to terms with another day. As you can imagine he never got further than the first couple of lines. I was too young, as was Davey, to remember Vera Lynn performing.

These were the cliffs that the Germans, when they occupied France, could see across the Channel, and planned to capture, but never did. They are the cliffs that became the symbol of British defiance against the German intention to invade. In the hinterland of these cliffs the most elaborate but well concealed preparations against that possibility were put in place. The cliffs, at the narrowest part of the English Channel, have great symbolic significance for Britain not only because of the German threat of invasion, but because of other similar threats in history. Julius Caesar mentions them in his account of the Roman invasion of Britain as far back as 55 BC, and Shakespeare refers to them in 'King Lear,' in commemoration of which one of them is called 'Shakespeare Cliff.' We had a wonderful view of these cliffs on a sunny mid-October afternoon from the deck of *Horncap*, when we sailed out of Dover harbour on the first leg of our five week voyage.

I had been on two previous cargo ship voyages. The first was in the mid-sixties when I was a student. A friend, Don, and I went as the only two passengers on a small cargo vessel, *City of Dublin*, from Dublin Port to Antwerp en route to Rotterdam to work for the summer as student helpers at The Mission to Seamen. The Master, Captain Dixon, was of the old school; he was not convinced of the value of modern electronic navigational aids and talked about 'radar-assisted collisions.' It was less than ten years previously that radar had been provided on merchant ships as a matter of routine. It was basic compared with radar today and crew already at sea had had no formal training in its use. Captain Dixon was known to his sea-going colleagues as 'Dynamite Dixon.' In dock in Belfast during the 1970s one of his crew was passing the security box at the gate of the dock when he met another seaman who asked: 'Who's aboard?' 'Dynamite,' he replied and went his way. The guard in the box overheard, phoned the police and the army arrived and took the ship apart!

Not long before we travelled to Antwerp on the *City of Dublin* a predecessor ship of the same name had been the subject of harrowing reports in the press when live horses it was transporting to the continent had died during a storm at sea. The Irish public was outraged that horses were exported for slaughter, and worse still that they should be shipped live in crowded conditions in a ship's hold where many of them had died in appalling circumstances. One evening at dinner the chief engineer asked us if we had ever eaten horse. We, of course, said we hadn't.

'Well you'll get it in Holland,' said he, 'it's like eating your brother.' Such is their love of the horse that many Irishmen would agree. How he felt about the scandal of the horses that died in the hold at sea, we didn't enquire.

Accommodation for passengers on board *City of Dublin* was basic. I slept in what at sea is called the ship's hospital; a simple cabin for a crew member who may be sick or injured. Don slept in the owner's cabin which, as you can imagine, was more comfortable. Every morning a seaman from the galley woke us with a large mug of tea. It was, however, so strong that it looked like tar and into it somebody had emptied a bag of sugar. It was simply impossible for us to drink it, so we both poured the tea down the sink careful to leave a little in the bottom of the mug.

Working at The Mission to Seamen in Rotterdam for a summer gave me some insight into the life of seamen. When in port they came to the Mission in the evenings to relax, play a game of table tennis and have a beer. Seamen spend their working life at sea and in foreign ports, very often with no time to go ashore. They are separated from their families for long periods, often for months on end and must cope with all the consequences of this for their family life. They live and work at very close quarters with other seamen and when not on duty they must be able to fill their time with some amusement or interest to relieve the boredom. They are, however, it hardly needs to be said, all individuals. They are as diverse a group of people as any other; they have their own reasons, hopes and aspirations and they have family problems and difficulties like any other group of people; isolation from family with more than average time to think can cause them extreme anxiety. It is interesting that in this way they share many of the problems experienced by prisoners.

My next experience of seamen and the sea was in 1970 when Hilary and I travelled as two of five passengers on a cargo vessel, *Inishowen Head*, to Montreal on our way to Chicago. A cousin of Hilary's, Frank, was Captain on a sister ship and suggested that since we had time we might enjoy the voyage. We did. We got on well with the other three passengers, two young women, Nancy and June, on the way to Canada on holiday and a young man, Chris, just down from Cambridge on his way to his first job with Oxford University Press in Toronto.

We joined the ship at Liverpool and to our amazement the chief officer was seasick for the first two days out. He told us that at the beginning of every new voyage he was sick but it passed after 36 hours or so! We found our three travelling companions congenial and we were free to go onto the bridge from where we looked for whale spouts, sea birds, other ships and anything else that might be of interest. We talked to the officer on watch and were shown the radar and how it worked (with all due deference to Captain Dixon), and how to read charts. One had some sense of the immensity of the ocean and how a ship must be entirely self-sufficient. We saw incredibly beautiful sunrises and sunsets. It was magic to be on the bridge during the black darkness of night, especially in the St Lawrence Seaway, when a ship passed in the opposite direction; the lights, the darkness and, above all, the silence. We learned at first-hand the meaning of the phrase 'ships that pass in the night.'

The chief engineer brought us on a tour of the engine-room during which neither of us understood much of what he was telling us. He was proud of his engine and at every opportunity he rubbed some part or other of the works with an oily rag from which he was inseparable. We also had access to the cabin of the radio officer, the sparks, when he was on duty. He was on duty in 2 hour shifts that covered 8 hours in every 24. He communicated by Morse with the shipping line Head Office, listened for navigational warnings, weather forecasts and possible distress calls from ships in the area. These days satellite communications are so sophisticated and everyday that the radio officer at sea is a thing of the past.

We messed with the Captain and officers, which is not what it may sound. In seafaring parlance which we were learning, it means that we ate with them. At meals we limited our questions to them to mask our ignorance of their way of life. They were patient and frequently amused at our naïvety. As you can imagine Nancy and June were popular with the young officers, and Chris and Hilary and I were invited on their coat-tails to officers' cabins for drinks before meals. We disembarked at Montreal and made our way by train to Chicago a few days later. It had been a wonderful experience that we never forgot.

Over the years we often talked about taking another voyage and we even cut from newspapers advertisements for cargo ship voyages and put them into a file marked 'Holiday Possibilities.' We were lucky to retire fit enough to spend some time travelling and eventually came round to thinking again about a holiday on a freighter. By now the internet made it easy to see what was available, so we booked for a five week trip on *Horncap*. From

Dover, the proposed voyage was to Antwerp and Le Havre to pick up cargo, possibly calling to the Azores, then across the Atlantic to the West Indies – Pointe-à-Pitre (Guadeloupe), Fort-de-France (Martinique), Cartagena and Turbo (Colombia), Moin (Costa Rica) and then back to Dover. *Horncap* is a sister ship of *Hornbay* and *Horncliff*, of a German shipping company, Horn Line of Hamburg. Together with two chartered ships they make the same run every week to bring back bananas, pineapple and other soft fruit to Europe. On the way out they carry a diversity of goods to the Caribbean.

In January *Horncliff* had been hit by a freak wave and crippled towards the end of a return voyage from Central America. The Captain was injured and when the weather allowed he was taken off the ship by helicopter and flown to hospital. Some of the passengers were slightly injured. The ship eventually limped to port at Falmouth. We had originally tried to book our voyage on *Horncliff* for dates in October but she had her full complement of passengers for that sailing, so we booked on *Horncap* for a week later.

The *Horncliff* drama at sea, though slight in comparison, reminded me of the newspaper and radio reports of sensational events which I remember vividly from my childhood. In December 1951- January 1952 in the same area of the Western Approaches *Flying Enterprise*, a freighter on a voyage from Hamburg to America was caught in a storm on Christmas Day. Her cargo of pig-iron had shifted causing her to list; shifting cargo is the great fear at sea, an even greater fear than fire. The following morning the list increased and the decision was made to abandon ship. Her lifeboats had been lost in the storm so her 10 passengers and her crew had to jump into the sea to be rescued by an American naval vessel standing by. Captain Kurt Carlson stayed with his ship, along with Kenneth Dancy, the chief officer of the rescue tug *Turmoil* who had gone on board. The conditions alternated between storm, gale and just foul weather. Eventually when it was possible to get a line on board efforts to tow her succeeded at first. However 40 miles from Falmouth they finally failed, when the list was such that Carlson and Dancy abandoned ship by walking along the partly submerged funnel and jumping into the sea before being picked up. *Flying Enterprise* went down shortly afterwards. These events lasted for a riveting fourteen days. At that time, before television brought such dramas into the living rooms of the nation, the people of Europe and, it is not an exaggeration to say, people throughout the world, were glued to every radio news bulletin to hear the latest on these dramatic events. For days on end the front pages of newspapers were covered with reports and photographs. The Captain's reluctance to leave the ship and the dramatic efforts to save her spawned all kinds of rumours that there was something contraband on board.

The one thing we were careful to do when arranging our voyage on *Horncap* was to book dates after the hurricane season in the Caribbean, not that nature is amenable to dates on a calendar. There is a jingle about the hurricane season which goes:

'July; stand-by.
August, September; always remember.
By the end of October
It should all be over.'

We had no way, however, of evaluating generally whether our planned trip was a good one to choose or not so I remembered a friend, Derek, from school days.

That which I remember most about Derek was that he had something, as far as his school work was concerned, that was markedly lacking in me. He had a quiet but dogged determination to pass exams in order to enable him to train for the career upon which he had set his heart since he was a small boy. His all-consuming ambition was to go to sea. There was nothing else in life that he wanted to do, and virtually everything he did was directed towards that end. No consideration would be given to bank, insurance, accountancy or any other career. Derek, come hell or high water, if you will excuse the pun, was going to sea. He paid particular attention to subjects that he would need for his marine exams when the time came. Not that the school gave the slightest indication of the reason for studying any particular subject. They didn't give even a hint that the study of some subjects was for the development of the person and that other subjects were the basis for preparation for training for a career in life. I used to wonder what farmers' sons, who were plugging in time until they went home to farm, thought was the purpose of reading Virgil in Latin or learning French poetry. Did some of the masters themselves think beyond the fact that subjects had to be studied because they were on the exam curriculum? If they did they kept it a secret. What they did know was that by one means or another, often violent, they had to coerce pupils to learn. With Derek no explanations and no coercion were necessary.

You didn't have to look far to discover the source of his ambition to go to sea; his father was Captain of *Lady Gwendolen*, which along with her sister ship *Lady Grania*, were two Guinness ships that plied between Dublin and Manchester. I was born and brought up in a port town, Wexford, where there were families that were known to be sea-going families and I knew that seafaring was likely to be 'in the blood,' so when I learned what Derek's father did for a living Derek's ambition did not surprise me.

Derek spent a good deal of his spare time reading about ships and drawing them and drawing the flags of shipping lines. I seem to remember that one of his favourites was the Blue Funnel Line, which sounded romantic to me, and which line it transpired that he sailed with later. When we started to learn trigonometry I remember him telling me that in the future he would have to learn spherical trig, explaining the importance to navigation of the curvature of the earth. I don't remember asking him questions about his future career and I myself hadn't the remotest idea what I might do. I was as uninterested in my future as Derek was committed to his.

We both left school on the same day in June 1955; we are now both retired and I have seen him only once, briefly, in the intervening 53 years. Another boy, perhaps I should have said 'oulfella,' who had been in our form at school gave me Derek's e-mail address, so before we booked our trip I sent him the details of our proposed cargo ship voyage and asked him for his opinion. His reply was unequivocal: 'Your planned voyage looks terrific and I envy you.' We booked the trip that day.

Derek also told me that for his first four years deep-sea his ship carried 12 passengers to and from the Far East. Having attached a photo of *Horncap* to my e-mail to him he identified her as 'a fast reefer (refrigeration ship) with a speed of 20 knots which is quite fast for a cargo vessel. The passenger accommodation is likely to be limited so you are bound to come in contact with the other passengers quite a lot.' A knot according to my dictionary is '(loosely) a nautical mile,' without saying how a nautical mile relates to a mile on *terra firma*, and why the 'loosely' I have no idea. Do they find it hard to be accurate in measuring because of the waves? How they measure at all when there isn't a fixed point I have no idea. Derek commended our plan to bring a stack of books and a laptop and suggested that we should also bring a supply of DVDs.

He advised: 'You will spend quite a lot of time at sea and reefers do not spend much time in port so make the most of any opportunity to go ashore. The ship's agent, there will be one in every port,' (traditionally like sailors' girls, thought I), 'may be prepared to organise excursions for you. The Captain may be prepared to radio ahead and set something up.' He made another suggestion: 'Learn about maritime navigation if you are interested.

Most Captains and watch officers in my experience will welcome you on the bridge especially if you show an interest in navigation and the running of the ship. Learn how to take a position from GPS and lay it off on a chart; learn how to read a nautical chart (believe it or not they are fascinating) and how to read a radar screen. Ships at sea spend 100% of their time on auto-pilot but, again if you are interested, ask if you can learn to steer. Steering a ship in calm weather especially at sunset or sunrise can be rewarding, but be careful, if you become too much of a smart-arse somebody will ask you to stand watch!'

Take an interest in the running of the ship - Yes. GPS, read a radar screen, steer the ship! I'm sure that what he said was good advice, however having tried to read a simple book on navigation my mind turned to porridge and I gave up before I got very far.

Derek went on to say: 'I hope this is useful. It is almost forty years since I was deep-sea and the whole scene has changed. But if you take an interest in the ship and make the most of your time ashore you should have a great time. Your itinerary looks very interesting and quite unusual.'

Since Derek lived in Dover, our port of embarkation and disembarkation, he invited us very warmly to stay a couple of days with him and his wife Jenny on our way out and on our way back. We accepted his invitation and I looked forward to meeting Derek again after all those years.

CHAPTER 2

We had planned to travel to Dover by ferry from Dun Laoghaire to Holyhead, by train to London and on to Dover, and to stay two nights with Derek and Jenny before boarding *Horncap*. It was mid October and in the previous week the Dun Laoghaire ferry had been cancelled because of bad weather in the Irish Sea. We kept a close eye on the forecast for the day we were due to cross, and decided that, since the high speed ferry was vulnerable to heavy weather, according to the best guess of the forecasters it was possible, if not probable, that the ferry would be cancelled on that day. We changed our plan and wondered if we had been too timid, but Derek with a professional judgment reassured us by e-mail:

There is no doubt in my mind that you are taking the right decision. I have also been watching the shipping forecast for the Irish Sea on Tuesday and it does not look good. The wind is expected to be 35 knots and while it is South West and behind you it is at the top end of HSS operating regime and therefore the chances of cancellation will be high.'

We flew to Heathrow and took a train from London to Dover where Derek met us at the station. I don't know whether life experience changes personalities or if who we are is formed in early childhood and stays essentially the same for the rest of our lives. Derek's e-mails to me over a period of almost a year before we met were entirely consistent with the person I remembered from school over 50 years previously. It remained to be seen how he had weathered physically. As a boy he was medium height, lightly built, with a shock of thick black hair that stood up. I remember Culverwell calling him 'porcupine.' Culverwell was the boy in our form who had the facility for distilling into a nickname some of the essential characteristics of a boy. Haven't you often wondered who first attached a nickname to somebody you know, that catches something of the essence of that person's appearance: 'Sparrow,' 'Bumble,' 'Mick,' 'Bunny'? In our form it was Culverwell. I suspected that Derek would not be fat and bald, and I was right; he was only slightly heavier, the retired greyhound build, and his hair was still thick but now it was grey. How he thought I had weathered I didn't enquire and being kindly by nature he didn't say!

We had two days with Derek and Jenny, when we all got on particularly well, which might not necessarily have been so. As you can imagine the first 24 hours was peppered with 'do you remembers' that soon bored the wives, but that passed and we were entertained royally. We discovered that Derek had spent 14 years at sea. He had his master's ticket and had spent some time as first officer sailing to the Far East with the Blue Funnel Line I remembered him talking about when we were at school. He came ashore when he discovered, returning home having been away on a voyage for 3 months, that their first child, Susan, didn't know him.

He was operations manager of a ferry company out of Dover and then terminal director of Eurotunnel at the Folkestone end where he supervised the design, construction and operation of the terminal before retiring in 1999.

We had booked our voyage almost a year ahead, and now the day finally arrived; we were excited. Derek drove us to the dock to join *Horncap*. On the quay a steward took our cases and we followed him up the gangway. He showed us to our cabin. There were two single bunks, one on the outboard, and one on the inboard of the cabin. They had raised sides to prevent the occupant falling out in a storm during the night! There was a dressing table unit with drawers and narrow wardrobes on both sides, a desk with lamp and phone, a desk chair and an armchair with cushions. The cabin was carpeted and there were two rectangular windows with curtains, one of which opened, that we thought we ought to call portholes, but they weren't round. I have since looked up 'porthole' in the dictionary and it says: 'A hole or opening in a ship's side for light and air or for pointing a gun through!' No suggestion that a porthole must be round, but I have a feeling they must be, so there were two windows. Everything in the cabin, except us, was fixed, and on the surface of the dressing table and desk there was a transparent rubbery cover to keep things from slipping off in heavy seas. There was a washroom off the cabin with shower, lavatory and hand basin. Altogether our accommodation for the next five weeks was very comfortable; far from the image one might have of a banana boat.

We unpacked and made ourselves at home. 'Passenger Information' that we had received before we left home advised that we should bring cassettes or CDs 'so you do not have to do without your favourite music.' We brought our laptop on which we already had music and with which we could play 12 or 13 films our son Ben had provided. He knew that it would be difficult for him to choose films from his collection that his old fogey father might enjoy, but he did his best; he did not, however, have 'High Society' or 'The Prime of Miss Jean Brodie.' As it transpired I did watch one of his selections, 'Cinema Paradiso,' through to the end and enjoyed it. Hilary's taste in films is more catholic than mine and she enjoyed most of those we watched.

The passenger information booklet of the shipping line also told us that casual clothing and flat shoes are best. On cargo ship voyages formal clothing is not required. It also said that it was wise to bring high factor protection sun lotion, anti-seasick tablets and some painkillers. They warn that there will not be a doctor on board, but crew have training in first-aid and that there is a ship's pharmacy.

Maritime Law requires that with more than 12 passengers a ship must carry a doctor. Consequently many cargo vessels have accommodation for only 12 passengers.

At 3.30 pm, still at the quayside, we found the passengers' and officers' mess for tea and a bun. There we met four passengers, all German, due to disembark at our first port of call, Antwerp, at the end of their five week trip. They had enjoyed their voyage

17

immensely. They had only one regret: the weather had been good for the whole trip; no gales or storms to add spice to their experience. As soon as they heard that we were Irish they asked if we could write out the words of 'Molly Malone' for them. We duly obliged.

We also met Vernon and Alice, a retired English couple, passengers on our voyage who had just boarded at Dover too. Vernon had been a teacher of English Literature and Alice a civil servant. They were seasoned cargo ship travellers; this would be their tenth voyage on a freighter. They had travelled all over the world on British, Danish, Italian, Polish and South African ships, and now on a German vessel. In the late afternoon we sailed out of Dover harbour leaving behind that wonderful view of The White Cliffs, bound for Antwerp on the first leg of the voyage that we had looked forward to for so long. When the pilot had left the ship and we were well clear of the harbour we went up onto the bridge. 'Passenger Information' had told us that we were welcome to do so. In fact it recommended the bridge as the place to get the best view of everything. The officer on watch was concentrating on marking a chart so we just watched as the ship made her way north-eastward through the English Channel, said to be the busiest seaway in the world. At one stage I counted 23 ships in sight and we were impressed by the array of dials, screens and electronic equipment available to the officer on watch to ensure that we didn't bump into any of them!

At dinner in the evening we shared a table with Vernon and Alice, the English speaking table, who regaled us with stories from some of their previous trips and we learned much from them about cargo ship voyaging. We had an early night and next morning we did what we did every morning before going down to breakfast, we went up onto the bridge to check the co-ordinates to see how far we had travelled overnight. We were almost at Antwerp. On the way in to our berth we passed through a lock. I have always had great difficulty with spatial relationships and also with how things work. Despite having had it explained to me more than once, I'm still not sure I understand why locks are necessary; how you can have two levels of water and why if the lock weren't there you couldn't just sail on. Like so many things in life I just accept it on trust from those who know better. Please, whatever you do don't try to explain it to me again; I believe you. Out on deck we had a great view of the whole operation and I was immensely impressed by the skill of the tug crews who manoeuvred this large ship in and out of the lock.

When we arrived in Antwerp shortly after breakfast, the chief steward announced that there had been a communication from Head Office in Hamburg to say that *Horncap* was to leave Antwerp to sail straight to Colombia and passengers would be brought by taxi to Dunkirk in France, stay a night at a hotel, all at the company's expense, and join her sister ship *Hornbay* which was due out of dry dock the next day. The taxis would leave for Dunkirk at

6.00 pm. This gave us plenty of time to go ashore and have a look around the city.

For our day in Antwerp the chief steward booked a taxi which brought us from the quay to the city centre. Having been advised to by Vernon, we went first to see the central railway station. It is a magnificent specimen of railway station architecture. It is known as the 'Railway Cathedral,' a landmark of Antwerp. Built at the beginning of the twentieth century, it has a vast dome above the main hall; the hall itself is extensively decorated with a variety of marble and stone. There are a number of diamond and gold shops which are part of the adjacent gold district. The platform and tracks, covered by the huge glass dome, are on three levels. A fine job of restoration has recently been completed and the American journal Newsweek has judged it to be the world's 4th most beautiful railway station.

It was a sunny autumn day so we rambled around the city centre, had coffee and then lunch outdoors in the centre of a large square. Needless to say Hilary checked out the shops and mid-afternoon we met Vernon and Alice by arrangement to share a cab back to *Horncap*. We gauged our return to leave plenty of time to be ready for our taxis to Dunkirk. When we boarded the ship the rest of the complement of passengers had arrived. They had been informed of the change of ship when they went on board. They were all German; two couples and three men.

We left the dock at Antwerp in two taxis at 6.00 pm bound for Dunkirk. Hilary and I were in the second taxi, the driver of which, when we finally arrived in the environs of Dunkirk, hadn't the remotest idea where to go. He stuck as best he could to the taxi in front but lost him a few times, and found him again with the help of his mobile phone. I had this wonderful feeling of not being concerned; that getting us to the hotel was somebody else's responsibility. This was a feeling we had many times during our five week voyage, that of freedom from care.

Horn Line had arranged a comfortable hotel for us and in the morning we received a message to say that their Dunkirk agent would see us at 12 noon. It was Saturday, market day, so after breakfast we went for a walk around the extensive market, the largest one either of us had ever seen. Stalls covered seven or eight streets, where could be found anything from a pin cushion to a side of beef; food, clothes, furniture, hardware, plants, flowers, stationery, anything you care to mention. There was even a butcher's stall that advertised horse meat stirring memories of *City of Dublin* and that student summer in Rotterdam. The most remarkable stall was one that had a surface of about 6 feet x 12 feet covered by haberdashery; Hilary reckoned that it would be difficult to find most of the items, apart from buttons, in Dublin.

We returned to the hotel at noon to meet the agent. He was extremely helpful and sympathised with us because our voyage had been delayed. He informed us that *Hornbay* would be out of dry dock during the afternoon and that taxis would collect us at 6.30 pm at the hotel to bring us to the quay. We assumed that she was in dry dock for a regular service. She may well have been, but we learned later to our cost that she was there also for another reason.

The taxis picked us up on time and brought us to board *Hornbay*. As a sister ship of *Horncap* she was of the same layout in every respect, and Hilary and I were allocated the same cabin, No. 3. We settled in and went down to the mess for dinner. There were three passenger tables: the English speaking one as on *Horncap*, the two German couples, Ernst and Carla and Hector and Sylvia, were at another and at the third table were Hartmut, Hubert and Albrecht. The Germans naturally spoke German together, but both couples and Hartmut spoke virtually perfect English, Hubert spoke a little and Albrecht had no English at all. The officers' table was across the mess from the passengers.

As the voyage went on Vernon and Alice and Hilary and I were fascinated by the formality of address the Germans used to each other. We called them by their first names, but to each other they were Herr or Doktor this and Frau that, despite sitting at table together four times a day. When we came to know Carla, who was lively and good fun, we asked her about this and expressed our surprise. We said that we hoped our informality of address had not offended them. She reassured us and told us that this was just the way in Germany. If, for instance, two couples sitting together got on well, after a period one of them might suggest using first names. This suggestion would come from the senior couple, but since in this instance both were on a par, a retired medical consultant and a retired nuclear physicist, either, or presumably neither, might make the suggestion. I didn't ask, but wondered in this kind of situation would the ones to whom the suggestion was made feel that the ones who made it, thereby felt they were the senior ones, and what if the couple to whom the suggestion was made said 'no'?' Germans also have the added complication of 'sie' and 'du' but excuse foreigners when they get this wrong. Such are the subtleties of different cultures that can only be really understood by being of the culture.

The crew, officers and men, numbered 26 in all. They were Ukrainian and Latvian, one Russian and one Moldovan. They communicated together in Russian. English being the language of the sea, the officers had to have enough of the language for their work, but for general conversation they had varying degrees of competence in English.

The crew member that we passengers related to for all our needs, questions and concerns was Alex, the Chief Steward. From Sebastopol, in his mid-thirties, average build, round face, he smiled readily and had some German and very little English. Every time we spoke to him in English he smiled and said 'yes' despite most of the time not knowing a word we were saying. When we had something of importance to say to him we had a better chance of being understood if we asked one of the Germans to say it for us.

Later that evening we sailed, cargo-less, back to Antwerp. We could only surmise that the reason the company had not put us up in a hotel in Antwerp for the two nights, was that the cost of the two taxis for 11 people from Antwerp to Dunkirk and one night in the hotel in Dunkirk was cheaper than two nights in a hotel in Antwerp. Next day we took on containers. We were not sure what they contained and neither was Alex. Crew don't always know what's in containers. Somebody said there were cars and other manufactured goods.

Containers are a relatively recent innovation for transporting goods at sea. The earliest ships to carry them were specially converted World War II tankers. The first purpose-built container ships began to operate in the 1950s. At the outbreak of the Vietnam War the American shipping company that carried supplies to the American forces in Vietnam used the conventional method of stowage in the hold; the way that goods had been carried on ships forever. A wide variety of supplies had to be stored in holds with due regard to compatibility with other cargo, ventilation, ship stability and sequence of discharge. Dangerous goods had to be secured on deck. This was a slow, laborious, labour intensive, sometimes dangerous and expensive process. The Pentagon told the shipping line that unless they could deliver on time, in order, undamaged, no loss from pilferage and at no additional cost, they would lose their business.

The shipping company devised a system of packing the goods into large metal 'boxes' on the quayside. The 'boxes' were of different sizes to accommodate different categories of goods. Larger and stronger cranes were fitted on the ships to handle the 'boxes'. This system worked well; there was little damage to goods, no pilfering and the method facilitated the discharge of supplies at different ports in the right order. It was a bonus that this also reduced significantly port labour costs.

In due course the size of containers was standardised, large purpose-built cranes were installed permanently on quaysides and of course containers were filled at point of supply or manufacture and not in the port. After some initial opposition by dockers' and seamen's unions and some port authorities, container traffic became a major success and transformed maritime commerce. Since *Hornbay* was a refrigerated container ship each container was connected to a central refrigeration system and there was also hold accommodation.

So, two days behind schedule, we sailed from Antwerp to Le Havre. On the first of our two days in port there we went for a day to Honfleur 20 minutes along the coast from Le Havre. It was the seaport of the region before Le Havre was developed. There was a plaque on the quay to commemorate Samuel de Champlain who set out from Honfleur in 1608 and founded the city of Quebec. It is a delightful town of great character. The extremely well-maintained 17th and 18th century houses of the harbour area, many of them slate-clad, are reminiscent of the merchant houses on the canals of Amsterdam. These houses were represented in the work of a number of the Honfleur School of artists who contributed to the emergence of the Impressionist movement. The most notable of these was Claude Monet. Today Honfleur is a centre of yachting.

Next day we went into Le Havre itself. During the German occupation of World War II it was devastated by British bombing.

Many historic buildings were lost, 5,000 people were killed and 12,000 homes were destroyed. After the war architect Auguste Perret oversaw the reconstruction of the city in the modernist idiom. In 2005 UNESCO declared his achievement a World Heritage Site. They described it as 'an exceptional example of architecture and town planning of the post-war era.' It is one of the rare contemporary World Heritage Sites in Europe.

We spent some time in the André Malraux Museum of Fine Arts which is known for its Impressionist paintings, in particular the work of Claude Monet and Eugène Boudin.

When we returned to the ship there was no word of when we were due to sail. A little later by chance Vernon bumped into the Captain and asked him. The Captain told him there was a problem; they were working hard to fit some part to the new refrigeration unit that had been installed while in dry dock. The part had come from Denmark and as soon as that was done we would be off. The Captain recounted that he was under terrible pressure from the owners as to when he would sail. I assume their concern was that he should make up lost time as sitting in port costs money. This highlighted two recurring themes of the voyage; the first was how closely the office in Hamburg kept in touch with the ship and influenced even operational decisions, all in the interest of saving money. Gone are the days when the Captain was 'Master under God.' The second recurring theme was that unless they were specifically asked, how little the crew communicated with passengers about what was happening. Alex did his best, but even he had difficulty sometimes securing information and often it wasn't reliable. Later in the evening he came into the bar and told us that the pilot had been booked for 2.00 am.

At 2.30 am a noise woke me. It was the gangway being taken up. Alex had been right; the pilot had boarded and we were off. I stood at the cabin window and watched. The ship moved slowly from the quay leaving behind the lights of the industrial dockland, the great cranes and other accoutrements of the loading and unloading of ships and the neat rows of containers standing on the quay. In the background were the lights of the town. We were heading for the ocean, hoping it would be kind, and the prospect of 12 days at sea before our next port of call. At breakfast next morning there was great relief amongst the passengers that at last after all the delays we were leaving Europe on our way to the Caribbean.

CHAPTER 3

We sailed south-west towards the Azores on our scheduled voyage to Guadeloupe, Martinique (West Indies), Cartagena, Turbo, (Colombia), Moin (Costa Rica).

As we passed the north-west end of the Bay of Biscay we encountered a force 8 gale with waves that caused the bow of the ship to rise and fall 20 or 30 feet, sending clouds of spray over the containers on deck and sometimes reaching as far back as the bridge. This was, to say the least, uncomfortable; we felt queasy and holding handrails on stairs and alleyways was essential to staying upright. The stewards put guards in place around tables in the mess to make sure our dinner didn't end up in our laps. Hilary, who is more prone to seasickness than I am, took her anti-seasickness pills and put on the elastic wrist bands that a friend had given her as a seasickness preventative. After dinner that night there was no lingering in the bar; all the passengers went to their cabins for an early night. I didn't feel the need of medication but went to bed early too. By morning the gale had passed. Neither of us had been seasick and although some of the other passengers had felt wretched, none had been sick either. The power of the sea was borne in upon us; we had experienced at first hand a 'gale force 8' that since childhood we had heard mentioned in shipping forecasts on radio.

When the sea was smooth the ship was boss and cut through the water and the sea had no perceptible effect on her forward momentum; the wave power being slight did not affect the progress of the ship. As the sea became angrier, at a certain point there was a turnover and the sea started to boss the ship; she started to pitch and roll which slowed her progress by three, four or more knots. The effect that wind has on a ship depends upon from which quarter it comes. Head on, the wind causes the ship to pitch and speed is reduced. This was what we experienced passing close to the Bay of Biscay. A following wind causes less movement of the ship and very little sea comes aboard. Beam on, which is from the side, is most uncomfortable. That's when anything that moves is secured and walking around the ship can be hazardous. The gale bore in on us something of the reality and the immensity of the achievement of people who circumnavigate the world alone on small yachts.

A day or two later Alex put us through a routine emergency drill with life-jackets and wet-suits in case of crisis. At the end of this exercise we watched a video in the passengers' lounge on how to evacuate the ship in lifeboats. The trouble was that the commentary was in Russian and none of us understood a word of it. Hartmut walked out in high dudgeon.

Passengers in the normal course of the day had contact with only some of the crew: the Captain and deck officers when we went onto the bridge, the chief steward and the two messmen who served at table and cleaned our cabins. We saw the chief engineer at mealtimes; he was a kindly man who didn't initiate a greeting when we met him, but always responded if we spoke to him. There were 2nd, 3rd and 4th engineers, an electrical engineer and a refrigeration engineer, but they didn't mess with the other officers. We had no contact with the other seamen apart from passing them occasionally on a stairs or alleyway. I have already introduced the chief steward, the crew member with whom we had most dealings; the smiling and affable Alex. One day, early on, the constant throb of the engine, always in the background, stopped for no more than five minutes before starting again. Later when I asked Alex what had happened he put his hand behind his ear, listened and said: 'The machine is machining,' meaning 'the engine is running.' We couldn't be sure if he hadn't understood the question properly, he didn't want to say what had happened or he didn't want to reveal that he didn't know.

The Ukrainian pipe-smoking Captain, in his late fifties, who had never sailed with passengers before, was a small square man with hair tightly cropped. Early on in the voyage in the mess one evening before dinner he came over to the passenger tables and shook hands with all of us. As he passed behind our table he kissed Hilary on top of her head, and when the rest of us tut-tutted he covered his embarrassment and ruined it all by saying: 'You remind me of my mother!' Subsequently we learned that earlier in the year he had had a tragic time. Over a period of months his wife and two adult sons had died, in what circumstances we didn't know. When things weren't going to plan his great phrase was: 'Don't worry, don't worry,' which I believe was a cover for his own stress in coping with the latest problem.

The Latvian chief officer was a different kettle of fish altogether. For the duration of the voyage he simply didn't talk to passengers unless absolutely necessary. He gave us the impression that he would have preferred if we weren't there. If we said 'good morning' to him he either ignored us or just grunted. We learned from the second officer that he had been chief officer on *Horncliff* when she had been crippled and her Captain injured. He took command and brought her into port. On the bridge on *Hornbay* most of the time he stood impassively staring ahead, left hand under right elbow smoking a cigarette. The first thing he did when he came off watch and into the mess was to drink a glass of milk. We surmised that he had an ulcer, and this wouldn't have surprised us as he presented as one of the unhappiest men in the world.

In marked contrast to No1, the second officer, Boris, was friendly. He was born in the Ukraine but now lived in Riga, Latvia. Although he was reticent with passengers at first, Hilary and I came to know him quite well. He had more conversational English than the others. He had done his compulsory military service in the Russian army as a tank commander. Then he went to sea as a radio officer and retrained as a deck officer when radio officers were no more. We always made it our business to go onto the bridge at some stage when Boris was on watch. He would smile and greet us warmly. As time passed he told us about his wife, his daughter and his granddaughter, and showed us photos of them on his laptop that he had on the bridge with him. For me it was reminiscent of that summer at The Mission to Seamen in Rotterdam as a student; most seamen, at the slightest opportunity, were ready to talk about their families. He also showed us a photograph of himself in the turret of a Russian tank. We were careful not to ask him indiscreet questions when something was going on onboard, but he was one of our sources of information when passengers were left in the dark.

Victor from Sebastopol, in his mid-twenties, was third officer. He too was friendly, but his conversational English was limited. Young and enthusiastic, he was often on the bridge when not on watch. He didn't mess with the other officers; we assumed he ate with the men. His wife, at home in Sebastopol, had had a baby since he left home and he looked forward to going ashore in Costa Rica to an internet cafe where he would be able to check his e-mails and see a photograph of his first child.

Vasyl was the assistant messman. In his early thirties, Ukrainian, he was on the crew list as coming from the 'Odessa region.' Not a word of English apart from 'boiled, fried, omelette' and 'thank you,' he was gentle, smiled and did his job well.

I have left the senior messman until last. He needs special treatment; he was the bête noir of the trip. I see from the crew list that his name was Pavlo; we knew him as 'Seven Thirty.' On our first evening before dinner all the passengers were in the bar, which was an open area beside the mess. We were having a duty-free pre-prandial, (Jameson €1 a shot, rum and liqueurs, 70 cent) and a chat. At a couple of minutes after half past seven, the stated time for dinner, he came into the bar and wrist in the air he pointed belligerently at his watch. Conversation was good and we were finishing our drinks when in another five minutes he came in and pointed at his watch again. At the end of the meal we were sitting chatting when he went across to the bar and put on some appalling music, as he thought to lure us away from the mess so that he could get on with clearing the tables. He behaved as though we were there for his convenience rather than that he was there for ours. Early on Alice asked him if she could have a second pillow. 'How much it worth?' he asked. Alice didn't reply, but he provided the pillow. Hartmut, according to his practice in similar situations, tipped him at the beginning of the voyage, but he did not escape his opportunism.

Le Havre to our next port of call, Guadeloupe, was a nine day voyage during which, except for passing the islands of the Azores, we were out of sight of land. As we passed the Azores we had a strong enough mobile phone signal to send and receive our last text messages to and from family until we returned to Europe. We were however able to send and receive e-mails while at sea.

As we went south the weather became warmer and the 3 x 4 metre dip pool on deck was filled. When the ship rolled, the water in the pool sloshed from one end to the other, but in the really hot weather that we had later on it was a great pleasure to cool down with a 'dip.' The pool was emptied and filled from the sea every day.

Between the Azores and the West Indies the weather was fine, warm and sunny and the sea was smooth. Before the trip we had wondered how we would get on with the other passengers during such a long time at sea. We needn't have worried.

Vernon and Alice, our companions at the English speaking table, were due to do the round trip, but on the way out they decided they would disembark in Costa Rica, spend a week's holiday there and return one week later on one of Horn Line's chartered vessels. As experienced cargo ship travellers they interpreted things for us and helped us to make the most of the voyage. Here I digress to give the substance from an e-mail that we received from Vernon after we arrived home about the ship on which they returned to Europe. It shows something of the variety of passengers and ships one is likely to encounter on cargo ship voyages.

When Vernon and Alice arrived at the quay to join their ship they met a rusty neglected old vessel, but appearances were deceptive. She turned out to be particularly comfortable and their cabin was well fitted. The previous occupants of the cabin had been an elderly Italian couple who had started in Argentina and were driving from Costa Rica to Alaska. Two of the other three passengers were a young Swiss couple who had been travelling around South America on motor bikes and ended up in Cartagena, Colombia, where they spent six weeks punching in time waiting for a ship that would take their motor bikes. The third passenger was a middle-aged German who had been on the outward voyage from Amsterdam and had gone ashore only at Guadeloupe and Moin. He had a mass of unruly blonde shoulder length hair, and wore a lumberjack shirt, blue shorts and sandals.

Back to, by comparison, the relatively staid and sensible passengers on board *Hornbay*. Ernst and Carla were booked to travel as far as Cartagena, Colombia, where they planned to stay a few days before meeting with their two daughters for an extensive tour of South America. Ernst, a retired nuclear physicist, was gentle and quietly spoken. He added statistical and technical facts, which he acquired from his visits to the bridge, to the store of information of the passengers. He even acquired information from the logbook, which I'm not sure would have been approved of by the chief officer. He would have been scandalised since he gave the impression of not approving of anything that passengers did.

Carla, a teacher of English, was always ready for fun. She was interested to know about English words and idioms that we used which were unfamiliar to her. She had an amazing haircut. One side of her head was shaved tight and the other side of her wiry fair hair was stretched across her head ending up in a bush at the other side, as though it had fled there to escape the blade. Hilary told me that perhaps it was the latest fashion. I can imagine Ernst's wry comment when she arrived home from the hairdresser!

Hector and Sylvia would be leaving the ship at Moin, Costa Rica, for a holiday in Central America. Hector was a retired medical consultant. He owned a yacht and had a good deal of knowledge of navigation and the sea which he was pleased to share with other passengers. He was particularly interested in what went on on the bridge and even kept an eye to proceedings there when pilots were on board.

Sylvia read a lot, but admitted readily to being bored much of the time. In the bar in the evenings she was pleasant company and enjoyed conversation which seemed to relieve her boredom.

Hartmut had spent most of his working life as commercial attaché to German Embassies in the United States, Spain, Mexico and Brazil. He had flown the Atlantic many, many times in his life and had come on the trip to experience what it was like on the 'ground.' He was a disciplined man and used the exercise bicycle and treadmill in the exercise room every day.

Tattooed Hubert was a retired seaman and was on the voyage because he wanted to spend some time at sea again, and since Albrecht was shy and had no English we knew almost nothing about him.

Time did not lie heavily on our hands. The human interaction between passengers and crew, ocean watching, the interest of navigation on the bridge, reading, the swimming pool and the day punctuated by meals filled our time with variety and we had the wonderful feeling of absence of care. The only responsibility we had was to do our own laundry and turn up in the mess at mealtimes.

There was a laundry room for passengers with a washing machine, tumble dryer, iron and ironing board. On the door was a permanent notice 'PASSENGERS ONLY.' Despite this Seven Thirty used it, we assumed for no other reason than that the main washing facilities for the ship's crew were in use much more of the time and it was more convenient for him to use ours. Furthermore there was a problem starting the washing machine that only he knew how to circumvent, but he wouldn't show passengers how to do it. When Alice asked him how he said: 'I do it,' which meant we had to find him whenever we wanted to start the machine. However, Hilary and Alice soon discovered the trick, but still had the problem of finding his sheets and towels clogging up the passengers' washing facilities.

Alex made his announcements to passengers at breakfast. He would enter the mess with a big smile and say cheerily: 'Gutten morgen, good morning,' and proceed to the matter in hand first in German, which apparently was not good, but understandable, and then in English, the gist of which we could usually deduce, but often had to clarify with one of our German friends what he had said. One morning he announced that there would be a conducted tour of the ship for passengers starting at 11.00 am, and who would be our guide but the chief officer? It was obviously a designated duty for him; it wasn't conceivable that he would volunteer to have anything to do with passengers.

We met on deck at the appointed time and were given hard hats. The chief brought us forward towards the bow of the ship past the containers on deck and gave us his spiel on the ship, the cargo and how passengers should comport themselves on a freighter. The trouble was that unless you were right beside him you couldn't hear a word. It surprised us that his English was as good as it was, but he was one of those people who seem to believe that because he had said something he had communicated. At one point he berated Albrecht who had wandered, away from the main party. To be fair to him it was because to have wandered where Albrecht had was unsafe. Having been right up to the bow he brought us back to the stern where there was what looked like a small container. It was a weather station from where every day a weather balloon was released that sent a signal back to the station which was relayed to a weather headquarters in Germany. When we arrived at the weather station the Captain was there and seemed particularly interested to explain it to us. We learned quite a bit on the tour and later one of the passengers claimed that at one point, for some reason unknown to us, the Chief Officer actually smiled. This was hotly disputed by the rest of us. The tour was one of a number of events put on for the benefit and amusement of passengers.

The Captain's dinner was the next such occasion. The Captain, chief engineer, second officer and second engineer attended in uniform, which they didn't normally wear. The evening was choreographed by Alex. Champagne was served in the bar before dinner, wine with the meal and unlimited vodka afterwards all on the 'house.' Oleg, the ship's cook, pulled out all the stops and provided a very good meal.

To be at sea for five weeks in the limited space of a cargo ship could be claustrophobic. For seamen voyages can last for months. Derek had written to me about his own time at sea:

'It was frequently necessary to go ashore just to get off the ship to get away from the noise of the generator the smell of the fuel mixed with the smell of cooking, bodies living closely together and often the smell of the cargo being carried, which on a general cargo ship ranged from stinking wet hides to delicately scented palm oil. It was also necessary sometimes to get away from your shipmates (or Board of Trade acquaintances as they were known). Imagine being locked in a factory or an office with your work colleagues for weeks on end.'

On *Hornbay* the noise of the generator and the throb of the engine were ever present, but after a while we became used to the background sound and didn't notice. There was no smell of fuel or cooking. Our cargo was in refrigerated containers so there was no smell of cargo. Perhaps for crew there was the tension of bodies living and working closely together but for us there was plenty of passenger space so that we could have company or be on our own as we chose. Furthermore the complement of passengers was congenial. We were all roughly of an age, that of early retirement, and Hilary and I found our fellow voyagers good company.

We had been brought up in neutral Ireland during World War II, and although we both had uncles on active service, the war was remote from us. Ernst, born in January 1945, told us that his father had been taken prisoner at the end of the war and he hadn't seen him until he was released and returned home three years later.

Hartmut recounted how at the end of the war the Americans had requisitioned his home and were billeted there for a time. His family went to live with his grandparents. He remembers, aged nine, going back to his house from time to time when the American soldiers were kind to him and on one occasion gave him a banana, the first one he had ever seen. He could not have known that in his retirement he would voyage across the Atlantic and the Caribbean to accompany thousands of tons of bananas back to Europe. When his family returned to their home he discovered a revolver in a drawer, but the Americans were soon back to collect it!

Both Ernst and Hartmut told us stories of the risible surveillance to which Eastern Bloc scientists and diplomats, with whom they had had dealings, were subjected during their professional lives. During his time in Brazil Hartmut saw the children of communist diplomats taken from a swimming pool because they were playing with the children of Westerners. All these things were to us firsthand accounts from life of a kind that was outside our experience.

Another diversion for the passengers: a tour of the galley. Again choreographed by who else but Alex? This was his area of special responsibility. Passengers assembled in the mess. He provided each of us with a paper chef's hat and a glass of wine, and led us through the door from which our meals emerged and at which Seven Thirty would stand facing us while we ate, back to one door jamb, hand high up on the opposite one, ready to whip away our plates as soon as we had finished. Alex led us down a short passage and introduced us to diffident Oleg, the Ukrainian ship's cook, and smiling Dymitro, from Latvia, his assistant. Later on, one day we met Dymi on the stairs and stopped to talk. His English was quite good. He told us he had a law degree but at sea he was certain of work and earned a good wage.

The cook must provide good quality meals and a reasonable variety as food will become the first focus of discontent on an unhappy ship. In the galley the cooker rings had guards around them to stop pans sliding off in heavy weather. From the galley Alex brought us into his domain, the pantry, where the ship's provisions were stored under lock and key. There was a cold room with meat and fish, a chill room with fruit and vegetables and a store of dry and tinned goods. In the past a dishonest chief steward could make a tidy sum in cahoots with his suppliers ashore. He would place an order for more than he needed, for which the supplier invoiced the company. Only what was needed was supplied and the supplier and chief steward shared out the cost of the balance. This was a well-known ruse which has been abolished by modern stock control systems.

Food on board was adequate. Oleg and Dymi, despite not having had advance warning, did well for Hilary and me as vegetarians, except that cucumber, which I cannot stand, appeared in one guise or another with provocative frequency to the point it became a joke with the rest of the passengers; they even pointed out a large supply of them in the pantry. For all of us the menu became repetitive after a while. Breakfast was best; juice, fruit, cereals, cheese, sliced meat, eggs any way you wanted (unless Seven Thirty was being particularly contrary), fresh rolls, tea and coffee.

After fourteen days at sea we look forward to our first landfall. As we travel south-westwards the weather becomes warmer. I stand on deck in hot sun, 360 degrees of smooth, blue ocean stretching to the perceptibly curved horizon. No sound but the throb of the engine and the swish of water along the side of the ship. No responsibility, not a care in the world and I think of the Park at home as the day stirs into action and the neighbours' morning routines begin: children going off to school, Jack setting out on his daily amble, Evelyn bringing Toby for his morning walk, Reuben cycling to work, others making for the bus or driving cars to brave the rush hour traffic. Here on deck, nothing disturbs the peace and tranquility; not another ship in sight on this vast disc of quiet blue water as we sail to the West Indies, full steam ahead in the heat of the day under a cloudless sky.

CHAPTER 4

For me the West Indies has strong associations with my childhood. When I was a boy cricket was a passion. In the late 1940s and early 1950s I used to listen on radio to test match commentaries and my favourite team was the West Indies. I always wanted them to beat England and frequently they did. Those were the days of the golden era of West Indies cricket.

Cricket in Ireland is a minority sport and most people know nothing about it despite Ireland's relative success at a recent Cricket World Cup, during which lifelong, dyed-in-the-wool GAA men sat on high stools in pubs around the country sucking pints and watching Ireland's cricketing progress on television. National loyalty overcame their ingrained distaste for foreign games as they came to terms with the finer points of cricket and explained them to each other as best they could.

'It's boring,' is the comment on cricket that one hears most often from the uninitiated. This is a superficial judgment from people who know nothing about the game. It is a classic example of how a majority can be utterly wrong. Cricket is one of the most fascinating and absorbing games there is and much of the time rather than boring it is very exciting. However if you haven't played it, or been close to it, you cannot appreciate the finer points of the game, and there are many such finer points, which make it perhaps the most interesting and subtle game in the world.

Cricket has given many metaphors to the English language, illustrated by the following report of a fictitious AGM of one of our wonderful banks!

'The chief executive, having presented his report to the meeting, knew he was on a sticky wicket. Now he would have to field some questions from the floor. The first question had spin on it but he coped well by playing a straight bat. The second question, however, was a doddle and he hit it for six. He had not anticipated the next question and he was badly caught out. To his great surprise the last question was personally offensive and he was stumped for an answer. The chairman intervened and said to the audience: "such an 'ad hominem' question simply isn't cricket; you have had a good innings," and he drew stumps.'

The game was invented by the English who brought it to their colonies. It took root and became the national sport of many of them, notably Pakistan and India. In both of these countries cricket is not just a sport, it is a national obsession. Satchin Tendulkar, known as 'The Little Master,' one of the greatest Indian batsmen of all time and one of the top five or six who ever played the game, cannot leave his house without being accompanied by half a dozen bodyguards to protect him from being mobbed by cricket fans. On a visit to my cousin in Pakistan, who is married to one of the four Pakistanis who don't like cricket, one lunchtime we saw on a small patch of open ground in a commercial district of Islamabad three games of informal cricket in progress. Young men in their lunch hour had squeezed three wickets into the small space in such a way that they did not cross. How the fielders knew which ball to chase, and how somebody wasn't seriously injured by the balls, I do not know. On a train journey from Rawalpindi to Lahore as we passed villages we saw small boys in the most impoverished conditions playing cricket, improvising bats with sticks and wickets with cardboard boxes or anything else they could find.

In the 1950s the West Indies was a power in the land of world cricket. On the team of that time there were the three Ws; Worrell, Weeks and Walcott, legends in their own time and ever since; there were also two bowlers of renown, Rhamadin and Valentine. In more recent times Viv Richards and Brian Lara played for the West Indies. They were two of the finest players in the history of the game. In the 1940s and 1950s there was something particularly colourful and exciting about West Indian cricket teams. In those days cricket in England was played in a sober atmosphere hedged about with customs and traditions and with good behaviour. Spectators at test matches at Lords and The Oval dressed soberly and sat silently watching and clapping sedately from time to time. Spectators at test matches in Trinidad or Barbados dressed colourfully and couldn't sit still. They clapped to the accompaniment of steel bands and sang calypsos during the match: 'Cricket, lovely cricket in the West Indies. / Although the day was dryer, Ray opened with Stolmeyer.......'

The islands of the Caribbean that make up the West Indies are divided into the Greater Antilles and the Lesser Antilles. The Lesser Antilles are divided into the Leeward Islands and the Windward Islands. Our first port of call was at Pointe-à-Pitre on the island of Guadeloupe, one of the Leeward Islands and our second at Fort-de-France on the island of Martinique. Both islands are French. They are overseas départements of France and as such they are integral parts of the French Republic. They elect representatives to the French National Assembly and Senate. Both islands are therefore part of the European Union and their currency is the euro and they are featured on euro currency notes. If you look at the bottom left hand side of the reverse of a euro note beside ΕΥΡΩ, the Greek version of euro, you will see a tiny map of French Guinea on the north east coast of South America and some islands that are French overseas départements; two of these islands are Guadeloupe and Martinique, our two ports of call.

Having told you all the foregoing about the West Indies and cricket, I must now tell you that Guadeloupe and Martinique are two of the few islands in the West Indies where cricket is not played. This is understandable. There is something incongruous about the French and cricket. It's hard to imagine that nation, much of the history of which has been lived at variance with England and all things English, including an obsession to keep English words out of the French language, playing that English sport! You can just about imagine Germans playing cricket (Der Cricketspiel); after all the Dutch, their linguistic second cousins, play the game.

You can even imagine the Italians playing cricket, without of course paying much attention to the rules, but it is impossible to imagine the French playing that quintessentially English game.

Guadeloupe comprises two larger islands separated by a narrow channel, and three small islands comprising in total less than 700 square miles. One of the larger islands, Basse-Terre, is rough and volcanic, while the other, Grande-Terre, has gentle hills and flat plains. The capital is the town of Basse-Terre on the island of the same name. Pointe-à-Pitre, the port for which we were headed, is on Basse-Grande on the narrow channel dividing the two islands. The total population of Guadeloupe is just under half a million people three quarters of whom are black or mulatto, ten per cent white and the rest of other ethnic origins. The official language is French and most of the inhabitants also speak Creole.

Christopher Columbus, on his second trip to the New World in 1493, was the first European to land on Guadeloupe. He was looking for fresh water and didn't leave any settlers there. The French took possession of the islands in 1635 and killed many of the native Indian population. During the next hundred years the English took Guadeloupe a number of times, only for it to be taken back by the French. Finally France ceded to the English their claim to Canada in exchange for control of Guadeloupe. After the French Revolution the upper classes refused to obey the new laws of equal rights for the native inhabitants and tried to declare independence. This led to widespread violence between the monarchists who wanted independence and the republicans who wanted to stay faithful to revolutionary France. During the fighting a third of Pointe-à-Pitre, where we docked, was destroyed by fire. The monarchists were victorious and declared independence in 1791. Two years later a slave rebellion started and the monarchists invited the British to occupy the Islands. They did invade and occupied Guadeloupe for a short time before the French retook it and freed the slaves. The slaves turned on the slave-owners who controlled the sugar plantations, but Napoleon sent a force that defeated the rebels and reintroduced slavery, killing 10,000 islanders in the process. Soon the British again captured the islands and planned to give them to Sweden under some political arrangement, but in 1815 the Treaty of Vienna finally gave control to France. Whew! What a chequered, complicated and colourful history for a tiny land of 600 odd square miles!

Today the economy of Guadeloupe relies chiefly on tourism and agriculture. Most of the tourists come from France, and the former mainstay crop, sugarcane, has slowly been replaced by fruit and vegetables, chiefly bananas, a cargo of which we took on board. Lying in the hurricane belt, the economy and the islands suffer severe damage from time to time.

Guadeloupe has a rich literary tradition, which is disproportionate to its size. The poet Saint-John Perse who won the Nobel Prize for Literature in 1960 was born there. Guadeloupe's literary standing today is represented by some well known poets, essayists and novelists, most notably Maryse Condé who was born in Pointe-à-Pitre in 1934. She was sent to Paris to school at the age of 16 and then attended the Sorbonne. She wrote novels and plays on black consciousness, race, slavery, gender, colonialism and corruption. The one for which she is best known is 'Sègou,' set in the city of that name in Mali, West Africa, at the end of the 18th century when slavery and Islam were becoming forces to be reckoned with. In recent years she has taught in a number of prestigious universities and she has won several major literary awards.

Guadeloupe has also produced many fine painters and sculptors. Some well known top class footballers or their families came from the islands; perhaps the best known is Thierry Henry whose father came from Guadeloupe.

The neighbouring island, Montserrat, which is not on our itinerary, lies to the north. Christopher Columbus landed there on his second voyage and named it after a monastery in Catalonia. Since the mid 17th century it has been a British island except for a brief period during the American War of Independence when it was occupied by France. In the early 17th century a group of Irish settlers fleeing anti-Roman Catholic persecution on the islands of St Kitts and Nevis landed on Montserrat and settled there. Their descendants today have Irish names, speak Creole with an Irish accent, and the island celebrates St Patrick's Day as a public holiday!

We docked at Pointe-à-Pitre late at night. Before we went to bed we had been on deck and watched as the first land we had seen for nine days grew from a faint outline on the horizon to become a clear stretch of coastline speckled with lights. Then the pilot came on board and brought us into harbour.

We went up on deck again first thing in the morning. It was hot and humid. We watched while some of our containers were unloaded onto the quay which is an immensely skilful business on the part of the operators. After they have cleared containers from the deck, they are able to take from, or drop into the hold with apparent ease, these huge containers with only a few inches clearance at each end. There were already on the quay many hundreds of containers in rows waiting to be loaded onto ships or to be taken away to be emptied.

After breakfast Alex booked taxis to take us into Pointe-à-Pitre. It was much as we expected a small West Indies port town would be; an old and poor rundown French colonial community overlaid with many well-worn, and sometimes incongruous, accoutrements of the modern world. People moved slowly in the heat and dried quickly after wettings from sudden rain showers. There was much extravagant colour. Clothes, especially of women, umbrellas, canopies over stalls and shop-fronts were all of bright colours. The stalls at the market sold fruits, (some of which we had never seen before), vegetables, spices, flowers, clothes, paintings by local artists, homemade rum, and lemonade, the ubiquitous Coca Cola and many other items of all sorts. Along the waterfront there were fish stalls, selling a variety of fish and other exotic sea creatures. Women sold fruit, flowers and vegetables from boxes on footpaths, and carried baskets and boxes on their heads.

We sat for a while outside a small café watching the laid-back world of Pointe-à-Pitre go by. We had finished our coffee when Vernon and Alice arrived and ordered coffee too. The waiter took our mugs inside, rinsed them under the tap and served Vernon and Alice's coffee in them!

Having had perfectly adequate but repetitive ship's food for more than two weeks, we looked forward to having a good meal ashore. We discovered what must have been the best restaurant in town, 'La Canne à Sucre,' at the far end of the waterfront, with a fine view of the bay. We found Ernst and Carla, who had the same idea, already there. We spent almost two hours over a good lunch. When we were paying the bill our delightful waitress invited us back to the restaurant that evening to a Hallowe'en party. Declining sadly, we made for our rendezvous for the taxi back to the ship.

When we arrived we were surprised to find that the pilot was already on board. Freighters will not wait for passengers because sitting in port costs money. On this occasion we all arrived back ahead of the time Alex had given us, but then Alex wasn't in charge of the ship! This furthered a suspicion we had formed that there was something strange about communication between the bridge and the chief steward.

Vernon recounted to us that on one of his many voyages in Puerto Madryn, Argentina six of the passengers returned to the ship after a visit to a penguin colony to find their ship about to sail. The departure time had been brought forward. They presumed that the Captain thought that they would find their own way overland to rejoin the ship at Buenos Aires, the next port of call!

We sailed south overnight from one département of France to another; from Guadeloupe to Martinique, which is the only other French island in the Lesser Antilles. Perhaps it is best known as the birthplace of Napoleon's Empress to whom he is reputed to have said: 'Not tonight Josephine.' He was probably conserving his energy for conquering Europe! Earlier in their marriage he had written to her: 'I awake full of you. Your image and the memory of last night's intoxicating pleasures have left no rest to my senses.' He obviously wasn't preoccupied with military affairs that night. On the latter occasion he was still besotted by her, and on the former she had worn a bit thin, perhaps because she was by now barren and could not produce an heir.

Josephine was born Marie Josèphine Rose de Tascher de la Pagerie in Trois-Ilets, Martinique in 1763 into the family of the owner of a sugar plantation. Her family was well connected in French aristocratic society. Her aunt was mistress to Vicomte de Beauharnais and when he died she arranged for Josephine's 12-year-old sister, Catherine-Désirée, to marry Beauharnais' son, Alexandre. However, before Catherine was ready to leave for France she died. In order to secure the financial and social advantage to her family of marriage to a Beauharnais, Josephine replaced her younger sister. In December 1779 she married Alexandre and they had a son and a daughter. Their daughter, Hortense, married Napoleon's brother Louis whose son in time became Napoleon lll of France. Josephine and her husband were both arrested during the Reign of Terror after the Revolution. Alexandre was guillotined but Josephine was released.

While she was a widow, she had a colourful career as mistress to a number of French aristocrats until she met Napoleon in 1795. She was six years older than him and it's a good bet that she was taller than him too! Until she met Napoleon she had always been known by her second name 'Rose.' He disliked this name and called her by her first name 'Josephine.' 'Not tonight Rose' would not have sounded quite the same! Two days after they married, Napoleon left for Italy to command the French army. Many of his love letters to her from this period have survived.

Shortly before their coronation in Notre Dame in 1804 an incident occurred that caused one hell of a row; Josephine discovered her husband in the bedroom of one of her ladies-in-waiting. Napoleon was a bad egg in more ways than one. However they sorted it out and the coronation went ahead. When it became clear that by now Josephine could not give Napoleon an heir she agreed to a divorce. They remained on good terms until her death in 1814. 'Josephine' is the last word that Napoleon is reputed to have uttered before he died.

The population of Martinique today is approximately one third of a million. The north of the island is mountainous, including a famous volcano Mount Pelé that erupted in 1902 killing over 30,000 people. The south is flatter and has many fine beaches conducive to sun and sand tourists. The history of Martinique is similar to that of Guadeloupe. Its earliest inhabitants were Carib Indians. After European colonization, control of the island alternated between England and France. At the time of the French Revolution the history of Martinique is virtually a carbon copy of that of Guadeloupe. A rebellion of slaves, who worked on the sugar cane plantations, was put down. A civil war between monarchists and supporters of the revolution ensued including a massacre and a declaration of independence by the monarchists. A resurgence by the revolutionists led to an invitation by the monarchists to the British to invade, which they did. In due course the island was returned to France.

Martinique too has a notable literary tradition. Aimé Césaire, poet, who died in 2008, aged 94, was one of Martinique's most distinguished literary figures. He was a pioneer of black pride and consciousness as a student in Paris in the 1930s and a tireless opponent of colonialism. As mayor of Fort-de-France he worked to change Martinique's colonial status and to make it an overseas département of France. He was a deputy in the French National Assembly for over forty years. He came to literary attention in the late 1930s with the publication of '*Notebook of a Return to the Native Land.*' He was a founder of the 'negritude' movement to affirm the cultural identity of black Africans. In his poetry he articulated the degradation of the black population of the Caribbean. President Sarkozy, whom Césaire once refused to meet when he was interior minister, over the issue of colonialism, travelled to Martinique to attend his funeral. As recently as 2007 an earthquake registering 7.4

on the Richter scale was recorded on the island. Like Gudaloupe, what with rebellions, civil war, a massacre, volcanic eruptions and earthquakes, life on Martinique over the centuries has not been dull. The capital of the island is Fort-de-France, the port where we docked to pick up a cargo of fruit. We had a few hours to go ashore.

Our taxi arrived at the ship at 9.00 am. We had strict instructions from Alex to return by 12 noon. After our experience in Guadeloupe we were determined to be back early. The date was 1st November, All Saints Day, a Church holiday, so all the shops were closed. The taxi driver dropped us close to the Cathedral, which in European terms was a large church. The day was fine and very hot and the big doors were open. Mass was just over, the organ was still playing creating a wonderful atmosphere, and inside and outside people dressed in their Sunday best were standing around talking. They wore plain and sober colours, and many wore white, the colour of respect for the dead in this and many parts of the world.

We rambled around the town and looked for somewhere to have a cup of coffee. Eventually we found a small restaurant attached to a hotel. There we fell into conversation with a French woman, probably in her early forties, who was a ramp supervisor at Charles de Gaulle airport, Paris. She was waiting for friends to arrive from Guadeloupe. She was besotted by Martinique and spent any free time she had there. She told us that dealers came from Guadeloupe to Martinique regularly to sell drugs. Later on as we wandered away from the centre of town a woman, obviously knowing we were visitors, crossed the street to warn us: 'Go back, pickpockets, pickpockets,' she said.

Hilary needed to get cash to use in Costa Rica. As the banks were closed we looked for a hole-in-the-wall cash dispenser and couldn't find one. We turned a corner and saw a woman in uniform coming towards us. As she approached I could see that, in her early thirties, she was, without doubt, the most beautiful police woman in the world. She was a little below medium height, lightly built, of mixed race with sallow complexion, and jet black hair pulled tightly off her face. She was smartly presented in her blue uniform. I approached her and asked if she could direct us to a cash machine. She smiled and told us to come with her. We accompanied her 30 or 40 yards to a turn on the right, where she brought us a short distance down the street to a cash dispenser. She stood at the edge of the footpath while we negotiated the machine and when Hilary had put her card and money away she smiled, bade us goodbye, went on her way and 'she with the walk of a queen.'

We arrived back to the Cathedral in good time to meet our taxi. There was another mass in session, the big doors were still open and the ethereal organ music wafted into the square outside. Our fellow voyagers arrived and the taxi had us back to the ship in good time. Our next port of call was Turbo, Colombia, down in the corner where Central America meets South America.

Shortly after this, hurricane Paloma began to appear on the navigation chart on the bridge. It was tracking at a distance from us, but in the general direction in which we were sailing. We were never close to it, but it was clear that we were keeping a weather-eye on it. As the track of hurricanes, once they become established, is fairly predictable, towns in their path can batten down the hatches or evacuate against their destructive force; the kind of devastation we sometimes see on our televisions. Unlike towns, ships can move and stay away from the path of hurricanes and wait until they pass. The worst they can do to shipping that avoids them is cause delays and thereby cost the owners money. At sea it seems nobody has sympathy for ship owners! If however a ship is caught in a hurricane it can do devastating damage or even worse, cause the ship to founder.

CHAPTER 5

One morning Alex came in to breakfast and after his usual cheery 'Guten morgen, Good morning,' he announced a tour of the engine room for passengers. Now engines are a matter of taste. Under the bonnet of my car I know that there are two important holes; one for oil and one for water. I know which is which and I don't know much more about engines. Having nothing else in particular to do that morning I thought 'why not?' All the passengers except Hilary and Carla came on the tour, which the chief engineer conducted. We were issued with hard hats and earplugs. Between the noise of the engine and our ear plugs, we couldn't hear much of what our guide said. Hector, who had a booming voice, seemed to have a good deal of knowledge about engines and was ready to share it. It didn't surprise me that the fitters and motormen who spent their working day in temperatures well over 100 degrees Fahrenheit kept their boiler suits open to the waist and wore nothing underneath. There must be easier ways of earning a living than spending your working day in the bowels of a ship, in those kinds of temperatures, often in heavy seas, with the constant noise of the engine. How anybody could understand all of the works that were down there I have no idea. I did understand that ultimately all of the equipment was in the interest of turning the drive-shaft that turned the propeller that drove the ship and as long as somebody kept the engine going, which as it transpired later on for a short time they didn't succeed in doing, we would be all right.

The chief engineer was quietly spoken and gentle but he would not greet passengers or speak unless we spoke first, despite meeting him at meals and around the ship. This was also the case with other members of the crew. It was something more than lack of confidence in conversational English. Nor could they all have been shy by temperament. Was this social custom in their countries? Was there a problem with crew relating to passengers? Was it that these men had lived their childhood, the formative years of their lives, and into their thirties or longer under communism? When anything out of the ordinary happened nobody mentioned it. Even when the engine stopped and we asked Alex what had happened his answer was to listen and give us his customary "machine is machining" response by which we knew he meant that the engine was running okay. Either he didn't know or he didn't want to comment.

On Eastern Bloc ships before the fall of communism in 1989, between the Captain's and the chief engineer's cabins there was the cabin of the political commissar; the communist party official on board to make sure that nobody stepped out of line. It was also likely in those days that there were party members amongst the crew who were ready to inform on others. The Captain told us that before 1989 he never progressed in his career at sea because he wasn't a party member.

Furthermore on *Hornbay* these men had to work together to get this ship to South and Central America and back. Crews are recruited by a shipping line from an agency for their three or four month contracts and almost certainly do not know each other before joining the ship at the beginning of a voyage. The Captain and chief engineer who met for the first time when they joined *Hornbay* discovered that they lived a couple of streets from each other in Odessa. It must happen often that two members of crew on a long voyage, sometimes as long as three months or more who must work closely with each other, simply by dint of conflicting personality which is the fault of neither, find it difficult to work together.

The Captain told Vernon that when we arrived at Turbo it was perfectly possible that he would get an order to join another ship somewhere in South America and a new Captain would take over *Hornbay*. This in fact did not happen.

Even when the unexpected happened, and on this voyage there were a number of unexpected events, the crew didn't speak about them. Passengers were told nothing. Was it a case that this had been the way of it with these Eastern Europeans for so long: you don't know who you're talking to, so say nothing and you can't get into trouble? Boris, the second officer, when we came to know him and when he relaxed with us, told us how he remembered well the first time after 1989 that he felt free to talk to passengers when they spoke to him. Now, however, it was 20 years since the fall of communism. Were these men conscious that they were doing the job for considerably less than western seamen would work for and that that was the only reason they were there? Or was it a case that they felt somehow disadvantaged because of their years under communism and now they were mixing with passengers who had not had to endure the same deprivations, but grew up with freedom, and had lived all their lives with 'goodies' of western capitalism. It is likely that these marine officers had been naval or military officers and had had to keep their thoughts to themselves and toe the party line and what that did to them when they had access to the West and saw a different way of life, is impossible for us to understand. I'm still not sure about all of this. Apart from the chief officer and Seven Thirty the crew did warm a little towards passengers as the voyage went on.

We were now well into the Caribbean travelling south west and the weather was becoming hot. Our cabins and other indoor areas were air conditioned so we could always have a swim or retreat inside to cool down.

One morning Alex after his usual bilingual greeting at breakfast had another announcement to make. That evening there would be a barbecue on deck for the whole ship's company; officers, men and passengers; a potential 36 people. However some of the crew would have to remain on duty to be sure we stayed afloat and on course.

The barbecue stood against one side of the ship and a long trestle table was erected athwartships, (How's that for maritime nomenclature? It means across the deck from side to side), covered with a brightly coloured, flowery, plastic 'tablecloth.' The Captain sat at one end with passengers and officers while crew sat down the table towards the other end. As we stood around waiting to sit down we saw crew members that we had never seen before and didn't see again. I give you one guess as to who the Captain invited to sit beside him. Yes, you got it; his 'mother.' I was careful to sit beside her! There was meat, sausages and smoked salmon for the carnivores and vegetarian sausages and kebabs for us, numerous salads, baked potatoes, cheese, bread and a variety of fruit to follow. There were jugs of beer, bottles of prosecco and cans of soft drinks 'ad lib' on the table. Oleg and Dymi had done us all proud whether Horn Line knew it or not.

After the meal the Captain invited Hilary and me back to his cabin for a drink. He showed us some photographs of his wife who had died recently, some of previous ships he had been on, of his dog that a friend of his wife was looking after and a monkey and a cockatoo that he had had in the past. He was a lonely bereft figure, but without a hint of self-pity, coping gallantly and determined, as he said himself, to finish out his life at sea.

Next day we passed along the coast of Colombia and saw in the distance Cartagena where we had been scheduled to call but didn't, with great inconvenience to Ernst and Carla who were due to disembark there. We were heading for Turbo, Colombia, which country's associations in the minds of Irish people are drugs and the links of the IRA with the FARC guerrillas. I needn't tell you that at Turbo we saw nothing of anything to do with FARC, but we saw thorough measures to protect the ship from the infiltration of drugs.

When we arrived at the port we did not berth at a quay; we anchored outside in the bay and waited our turn to be unloaded and loaded. It was dark. We said goodbye to Ernst and Carla as they went over the side and descended precariously the accommodation ladder with the pilot, boarded his motorboat and disappeared into the night. Horn Line had arranged for them to stay in Turbo and in the morning to fly to Medellin and from there to Cartagena the following day. They lost a couple of days of their planned holiday in Cartagena. Yet another occasion of extra cost for the company incurred by commercial considerations which caused change of plans that took precedence over the expectations of passengers.

In the harbour in Turbo Alex pulled the curtains in all the passenger accessible areas and asked us to draw the curtains in our cabins and to lock them. All the doors of the poop, (the superstructure towards the stern of the ship, the top deck of which is the bridge) except one door from the wheelhouse to a wing of the bridge, were locked. There was a long delay before our turn to load; the Captain spent a lot of time on the bridge pacing up and down and you could cut the atmosphere with a knife. I have no doubt that Hamburg was putting pressure on him to get on and the delay was out of his hands. He was constantly under this kind of pressure from Head Office. Modern communications and tight commercial considerations mean that increasingly ships are managed from Head Office, often from the other side of the world.

Eventually the first people to come on board arrived. They were four uniformed security men with automatic weapons slung across their shoulders, with a sniffer dog. Later in the mess Vernon asked me if I had seen the dog. I said I had and that I assumed he was there to sniff out drugs. Alice came back like a shot:

'He's hardly going to load bananas!'

After we were home we received an e-mail from Ernst and Carla in which they recounted that there had been an article in their local newspaper saying that in Bavaria a supermarket had opened a box of bananas, from Colombia via Antwerp, to find under a top layer of fruit 28kg of cocaine worth 10 million euro. Some dog on some ship must have been loading bananas when he should have been sniffing drugs!

The security men stayed on board for the duration of our time in port, and slept overnight in hammocks that they slung anywhere they could. In the morning tugs arrived carrying dockers and pulling lighters onto which to unload. The security men stood at the top of the gangway and searched thoroughly all of the dozen or so dockers before allowing them on board.

Loading and unloading the ship usually took place when passengers were ashore so we saw little of it, but since here it was taking place out in the bay we watched the operation from the bridge. At a quay the giant cranes did the job, but here the ship's own derricks were used. The whole operation is a highly skilled business with men climbing ladders to get to the top of containers and jumping from one container to another to attach the lifting equipment. When the containers had been unloaded from on top of the holds, the huge hydraulically powered covers were opened and pallets of fruit, mainly bananas, were lowered into them. It was hot, humid and enervating weather and the dockers seemed to work sporadically. They took breaks for grub that was supplied from a small motorboat that lay alongside while they were on board.

There were fax machines on the bridge that spewed out short summaries of world news at intervals during the day. I kept away from them for reasons I will give shortly, but Hilary read them from time to time. While we were at Turbo she learned from one of them that Barack Obama had been elected President of the United States. There was a number of these fax machines, one with Latvian news in English, and one that was devoted exclusively to maritime news, from which we learned of piracy off the Horn of Africa. Hilary said to the officer on watch: 'I see that some of those pirates have been shot.' 'Good,' said he. We could understand how at sea a ship was vulnerable to a gang of heavily armed men arriving on fast speedboats with evil intent. In the Caribbean, it seems there was no recent history of piracy as there had been in the past, à la 'Pirates of the Caribbean,' one of the films that our son had given us for the voyage!

One of the great bonuses of being at sea for me was being away from the news. In the middle of the ocean we were remote from the media that ashore bombard us every day with news that is 95% bad or tragic and certainly depressing. Most of it is written to fill the morbid prurience deep in the human psyche that wants to know bad news: wars, famines, atrocities, injustice, murder, rape, incest, all kinds of other crime, and all manner of human misery and depravity. It had recently become known that the banks were in a state of collapse, and the economy was on its way into deep recession. Depressing news sells newspapers and attracts listeners so that the media companies can sell advertising space and time in order that they and the advertisers can make money. The tabloid press does it in a gross way designed to appeal to the baser instincts of the masses while the so called quality newspapers do it in a rather more balanced and subtle way to appeal to the same base instincts of those who consider themselves more sophisticated. Both print and broadcast media are doing the same thing; they are filling column inches or air time to sell newspapers or keep audience figures up, by appealing to people's fascination with other people's suffering. At the end of an item on commercial television news last spring giving up-to-date information on an earthquake in China in which hundreds of thousands of people were killed, the presenter announced that further pictures of the devastation were available on the channel's website. Why would any decent human being want to look at more pictures of the destruction of towns and villages and the suffering and death of thousands of their fellow human beings? Maybe it is a case of the viewer feeling, 'I'm lucky not to be one of those unfortunates.' Or 'At least I'm not as badly off as those people.' The kind of thing that people feel at funerals: glad that they are not the one in the box.

For whatever reason many of us are in thrall to the media; it is easy to become a news junkie; news at seven, again at eight, 'What the papers say,' a daily newspaper, news at 1.00 clock, evening paper, six o'clock news, main evening news, late night news and start the cycle all over again next morning. What does it add to our lives to hear of all this pain and suffering? Would we not be better, rather than listening to the woes of the world, to do something that will nourish our spirit rather than depress it; read poetry, listen to music, or we could read history or fiction and discover that nothing changes? The world has been ever thus; human lives begin with joy and expectation and end in, at best, sadness or, at worst, tragedy. We don't want to deny the realities of life, but neither do we want to allow them to weigh us down.

Out on the ocean under the sky, if you stay away from the fax machines on the bridge there is nobody to bombard you with news of the human misery and human tragedy of the world. What of it for us if more people have been killed or maimed, if thousands have died in another earthquake, if somebody else has been murdered or more drugs have been found. We only need to know, if there is something we can do to help. What if the President of the United States has been caught *in flagrante* with a White House aid, the Queen of England has run away with a toy boy, or the

Pope has eloped with a chorus girl, and we don't hear these gems of prurient interest which would fill acres of newsprint and hours of air time? That we haven't heard wouldn't change anything for these notables, and it certainly wouldn't change anything for us. We can do without knowing. As they say these days - too much information. Out on the ocean we can enjoy the quietude, contemplate the immensity of the universe, the vastness of the ocean and the depth of the mystery that surrounds us. We can learn to cultivate that state recommended by Robert Louis Stephenson in his essay, 'Walking Tours:'

'To sit still and contemplate, to remember the faces of women without desire, to be pleased by the great deeds of men without envy, to be everything and everywhere in sympathy and yet content to remain where and what you are. Is not this to know both wisdom and virtue and to dwell with happiness?'

This state of contemplation is a far cry from the obsession of the news junkie. Which of these two, the news junkie or the wearied walker at the end of his long day, will be troubled and disturbed, and which will have his heart and mind fed and nourished? If there is a case to be made for reading a newspaper or listening to the news every day, I don't know what it is.

That which drives most things in society and makes possible the standard of living that we have become used to is the profit motive, which in excess becomes greed. Greed has caused the exploitation of people and the environment especially in the third world and contributed towards the deprivation, misery, starvation and death of millions. Earthquakes, tsunamis and drought have done the same. We can't lay the blame for the latter at the door of people who live by the principle of the profit motive. For these catastrophes nature is responsible.

On the other hand, if there weren't people who were motivated to make money; entrepreneurs, people in trade and commerce buying and selling we would all be in a bad way. There would be more hunger and deprivation in the world than there is. Entrepreneurs create jobs and prosperity, but the downside is that they exploit people and the environment. This is the great dilemma. Somebody has to keep a rein on them. Therefore some of the most important people in our society are trade unionists and environmentalists. It is hard to imagine the devastation of society and the destructive exploitation of the earth if entrepreneurs were given free rein. In Ireland, even with some constraints upon them, entrepreneurs and developers have plunged our economy into destruction, aided and abetted by those models of prescience, wisdom and moderation - bankers, encouraged by the self-effacing, self-giving servants of the people, politicians. All of them the elite of society that everybody looks up to, respects and admires, God help us all.

Then there are the parasites, in a non-pejorative sense; the professionals – doctors, clergy, lawyers and others. They don't contribute directly to the creation of wealth by manufacture or trade, but they service the people who do and to my mind, with the exception of clergy, are grossly overpaid and given excessive status for providing human services to society. What about artists, actors, poets, painters and writers? We need them to draw our attention to important insights about the mystery of the human condition, while singers and dancers entertain us in order to alleviate tedium and tragedy; to take our minds off life's appalling realities of pain and suffering in order to help us to survive.

Finally what can be said for the politicians already mentioned? Everybody has an opinion on them. Before coming to a conclusion we need to be aware that most politicians are drug addicts, addicted to the most destructive drug known to humankind – power. Like all drug addicts their view of reality is distorted. They don't see reality as the rest of us do. They see reality through their addictive need of the drug on which they are hooked, and consequently the damage they can do in keeping the channels of access to that drug open to feed their addiction is immense. It far exceeds the damage done to society by substance abuse addicts. The extremes of addiction to power can be seen in history in the person of people like Alexander the Great, Genghis Khan, Napoleon, and in our own time Hitler, Stalin, Pol Pot, Mugabe. Charles J. Haughey was a lesser specimen of the species. The damage done to societies by power crazy rulers and politicians is inestimable. The antidote to the addiction to power is democracy, not a perfect answer, but the best we have.

Nationalism is another dangerous drug on which many ordinary members of the population are hooked. Patriotism is an even more dangerous version of this drug that we don't hear so much about in these affluent days. Nationalism is the belief in the primary importance and promotion of the interest of a people who live on the same piece of land. They often share the same language and history and when there has been a history of invasion or occupation by another nation it makes this addiction worse. It leads its victims to believe in their own superiority over others. It is a drug which can lead the addict to kill and maim and sometimes it leads to their own martyrdom. As with all drugs it is not only the addict that suffers, but their families, friends and innocent members of society.

The paramilitaries on both sides of the political divide in Northern Ireland were badly addicted to this drug, but like all addicts, if they were to survive they had to come off it. The antidote was democracy; the peace process. What a great pity these paramilitaries who caused the deaths of over 3,000 people and maimed thousands more went on the drug in the first place. All the death, pain, suffering and destruction of 30 years would have been avoided if these addicts had supported the movement for civil rights led by people like John Hume. But then there is no blood lust, and there are no heroics or martyrdoms involved in working for civil rights. It is interesting to note that paramilitary drug addicts that end up justifying their murders on grounds of nationalism frequently espouse their Christian commitment. Yet Jesus showed no inclination to condemn, let alone to kill the centurion of the occupying Roman army, rather he healed his daughter. He also told a questioner to pay taxes due to the occupying power. He showed no inclination for nationalism, but rather his concern was for the wellbeing of people regardless of their social or political status or allegiance.

In Ireland in the popular consciousness there is an inextricable connection between religion and national identity; Catholicism and Nationalism on the whole island and Protestantism and British in the north. I am Irish and nothing else. I was born in Ireland, lived and was educated in Ireland, feel Irish, pay my taxes, and as a child and youth felt deeply about British involvement in Ireland. As an adult, however, I matured. I have become terribly impatient with people constantly affirming their Irishness, their Nationalism or Republicanism. Sinn Fein does it, Fianna Fail top brass marching solemnly to the Wolfe Tone commemoration at Bodenstown every year does it. I doubt if Wolfe Tone would have accepted large sums of money from business men. I doubt that he needed to draw lines in the sand or that he ever won unaccountable big money backing a horse. Politicians tip their forelock to Padraig Pearse and 1916 every now and again to affirm their Republican credentials. They want people to remember that that is what they are about rather than filling their own ego needs, massaging their expenses and feathering their own nests. The human condition is universal regardless of the colour of people's skin or the tribe or nation to which they belong or the boundaries of the piece of land upon which they live. However, people try to overcome their vulnerability by affirming in various ways their national identity inferring its superiority to others.

I was so frustrated and fed up last year with the Irish rugby team that I decided I would put to the test some of my thoughts on nationalism and that this year I would support Wales. I like the Welsh and the way they play rugby. Try it sometime! It didn't last long, and when it came to Ireland's last game against Wales for the Grand Slam I can assure you that my national loyalty was not in question.

Living in this world is about protecting our human vulnerabilities in order to survive. People do it in a myriad of ways, using a myriad of devices: nationalism, religion, politics, making money, striving for success professionally, socially, and in a thousand other ways. The trouble arises when we do it at the expense of other people. I often think of the writer Nuala O'Faolain who died recently. She presented as a warm, soft, gentle, feminine, honest and above all vulnerable, person, desperate to come to terms with the hurt at the heart of her life. If one had met her, the fear would have been of hurting her, and yet underneath she had an independent spirit, even a tough streak, that enabled her to survive. Her capacity to express publicly her most intimate feelings about her life, especially her relationships with people who were significant to her, and about death, in such a way as not to give reason for suspicion of a hidden agenda, was remarkable. She gave the impression of never having developed a permanent psychological device to protect her vulnerability, but to have continued to struggle with it. She was an admirable person.

Vulnerability is a theme of the early poetry of Brendan Kennelly. His poem *The Good* begins;

The good are vulnerable
As any bird in flight,
They do not think of safety,
Are blind to possible extinction
And when most vulnerable
Are most themselves.

The poem ends:

I think I know one or two
Among my friends.

You may disregard these ramblings and ruminations that arose from being in a state of suspended animation on a cargo vessel at sea. On the other hand to quote Jack Point in Gilbert and Sullivan's 'The Yeomen Of The Guard,' there may be 'a grain or two of truth amongst the chaff.'

Before we left Turbo divers inspected the underwater hull of the ship to make sure that drugs had not been attached.

CHAPTER 6

When we left Turbo we sailed along the coast of Darien which is the southern area of Panama north of the Colombian border. The name is familiar from the lines of Keats's sonnet *On First Looking Into Chapman's Homer:*

'Or like stout Cortez, when with eagle eyes
He star'd at the Pacific - and all his men
Look'd at each other with a wild surmise -
Silent, upon a peak in Darien.'

We, however, were on the Atlantic side of the isthmus.

We were on our way to Colon at the Caribbean end of the Panama Canal to bunker. I'm glad that mariners don't speak ordinary English; I love their maritime nomenclature. It means to take on fuel, and comes from the old steamship days when the fuel was coal and it was kept in a bunker. 'To bunker' is more romantic than the prosaic 'to take on fuel.' This stop was not mentioned in our voyage itinerary and as bunkering was done from a barge out in the harbour we did not have an opportunity to go ashore.

Panama was part of Colombia until 1903 when America supported their declaration of independence in order to conclude a treaty with them to give the United States control over the region that they needed to develop the canal. Colombia had refused to give them this permission. In the late 1800s the French had abandoned their attempt to build a waterway from the Atlantic to the Pacific. The Americans succeeded and the Panama Canal was opened in 1914. It was built through mosquito infested territory before medicine understood the role of the mosquito in spreading disease. It is estimated that between the French and American efforts 27,000 men died, most of them from malaria and yellow fever. A high proportion of these workers had been brought to Panama from the islands of the West Indies. This was a high price to pay, but the benefits to shipping are enormous. A ship travelling through the canal saves an 8,000 mile journey around Cape Horn. The United States did not finally hand over the Canal Zone to Panama until 1977.

We forget how cheap human life was in the past; especially the lives of ordinary people. I wonder how many of the 27,000 who died were 'big wigs.' Not many you can be sure. One way or another the 'big wigs' will have devised a way of avoiding disease, of staying alive; even though they didn't know how some of the diseases were transmitted. Such attrition of human life would not be tolerated today; the unions would close down the site until something was done, and rightly so. The benefits of the price that the 27, 000 paid has accrued to commerce since. It's hard to make sense of it all, as it is hard to make sense of war in which millions die and nobody wins.

On this part of the voyage we saw dolphins that swam for a short while beside the ship. I'm told that dolphins sometimes rub themselves along the hull of a ship to remove sea lice from their bodies. When we arrived at Colon, close to the Panama Canal, at seven o'clock in the morning the temperature was already in the mid-eighties Fahrenheit. There were about 25 ships at anchor between the bay and the harbour waiting to bunker or waiting their turn to go through the Canal. Our turn to bunker didn't come until the small hours of the morning so we saw nothing of the operation. Between waiting our turn and bunkering itself we spent 24 hours at anchor off Colon.

Next morning we sailed north of Golfo de los Mosquitos on course for our last port of call in the Caribbean, Moin, Costa Rica. After a few hours the ever present background throb of the engine stopped. Dirty diesel? I was on deck and saw that the sea was smooth where the wash had been. We were stopped, going nowhere, in fact we were drifting. I went up onto the bridge. There was no hint of alarm or even surprise from the officer on watch, who was alone. The phone rang. He spoke in Latvian or Russian. I looked at him as if to say 'What's happening?' He didn't respond. When he didn't react I didn't feel I could pursue the matter and went out on deck. Other passengers arrived and we seemed to be the only ones on board that were curious about what was going on. After drifting for about three quarters of an hour the engine started up and stopped. This happened a few times before, as Alex would have said, the machine started machining. We were on our way again.

That evening as we left the mess after dinner, Boris, the second officer, was alone at the officers' table. I asked him what had happened that we had stopped. Seven Thirty was hovering as he usually was, trying to hear what we were saying. Before Boris could answer he rushed over gesticulating and repeating 'No comment, no comment.' Boris ignored him and told me that he didn't know. On the bridge next day I asked Boris about Seven Thirty's behaviour. He replied gently: 'I spoke to him about it.' I have no doubt that a messman would not behave like this with an officer or with a passenger for that matter, on an Irish or British ship. I suspect that any messman anywhere, other than Seven Thirty, would not behave like this.

At this stage of the voyage passengers were curious to account for the strange behaviour of both the first officer and Seven Thirty. It was peculiar that the first officer wouldn't even say a civil 'Good morning,' and that Seven Thirty behaved as he did. (You will notice that we didn't have a nickname for the first officer; 'Grumpy' would not have been enough). We came up with the following theory that might be somewhere close to the mark.

At the fall of communism in Eastern Europe not every citizen was pleased to be rid of the socialist system. It is clear that there was a small minority of doctrinaire Marxists who bemoaned the demise of communism. In former Eastern Bloc countries still on May Day, Stalin's birthday or on some other such occasion, small groups of people carrying red flags or flags of the hammer and sickle make pilgrimages to some surviving shrines to communism. The chief officer and Seven Thirty may have been of this ilk.

They were Latvian and Ukrainian respectively so it is likely that they did not know each other before joining *Horncap*. However, and here is where our theory reveals its conspiratorial credentials, like the Freemasons' handshake committed doctrinaire Marxists may have some secret means of identification. Both men were in their fifties, so would have lived under communism for the first 30 years or more of their lives, and may have been activists who were now determined to co-operate as little as possible with capitalist pigs. Quite often when the first officer had come off watch and was alone at the officers' table, instead of standing at the door to the galley ready to pounce on our plates when we put down knife and fork, Seven Thirty would sit sideways on the edge of the chair next to the chief and they would engage in deep conversation. I have no doubt that Seven Thirty was an experienced apparatchik; at every opportunity he eavesdropped on conversations. In port on one occasion I turned the corner of an alleyway to find him listening outside a cabin door to a conversation between the Captain and the agent. Before dinner one evening in the bar passengers were in conversation with Alex about some matter to do with going ashore at the next port of call. I looked up and there was Seven Thirty standing between the bar and the mess.

'You're listening,' I said. The conversation with Alex went on, and Seven Thirty came right into the bar and said to me:

'How you know I listening?' I was about to say 'Because I saw your ears flapping,' and thought better of it; he might sabotage my dinner between the galley and the mess or I might end up overboard!

That is not the end of our theory. Seven Thirty, a messman who never said a word to us more than necessary to do his job, was in his fifties. Alex, chief steward, his immediate boss who was only in his early thirties was friendly, affable and helpful to passengers. A number of times Alex gave us information to do with times of sailing or docking or some such that turned out to be far wide of the mark. It was clear that somebody was feeding him false information, setting him up. Who was the most likely suspect? The chief officer, ably assisted by Seven Thirty?

This theory was reinforced one morning after breakfast when we were sitting in the bar, not drinking, I hasten to add, but in casual conversation with Alex, when the first officer came in. He spoke aggressively to Alex, and suddenly a vicious shouting match erupted between them in front of us. It continued for a couple of minutes, but since it was in Russian we didn't know what it was about. When the chief officer finally left, Alex, distressed, gave some account of the argument in German, which we gathered was that the chief officer had sent an e-mail to Head Office to report him for something. All that we English speakers heard at the end of this account was when he turned to us and bending down, cupping his hand behind his ear to indicate listening at a keyhole, he said: 'He crazy, he crazy, he very crazy.' These incidents went on in front of us; what went on behind the scenes we did not know.

Crew in general were more casual than I remembered from our last cargo ship voyage to Montreal in 1970. Officers on *Hornbay* wore jeans and tee-shirt on watch and wore uniform only on formal occasions like the Captain's dinner. The Captain was similarly casual but in addition to formal occasions he also wore uniform when pilots were on board. I don't know if things have changed at sea generally or whether East Europeans are less formal than others.

We berthed at the quay at Moin in the early evening; our estimated time in port was 36 hours. Next morning Hector and Sylvia and Vernon and Alice left the ship for their respective holidays in Costa Rica. Alex had told us well in advance that the rest of us would have time to spend the whole day ashore and that he could arrange either a trip up a river through the 'junglie,' as he called it, or a tour of a banana plantation. Hartmut, Hubert, Hilary and I opted for the jungle which was part of the Tortuguero National Park. Albrecht, who was stout, stayed on board. Hubert claimed this was because he had told Albrecht the crocodiles would like him! He had, however, stayed on board at some of our other ports of call with no chance of being eaten by crocodiles!

After breakfast Federico, our guide, was waiting for us on the quay with a minibus and Oscar the driver. It was only ten minutes to our departure point for the trip. Our boat was small, aluminium with a canvas canopy and outboard motor, driven by a friendly driver, leaving Federico free to spot for us the wildlife of the jungle. Under a deep blue cloudless sky we set off up the river with lush vegetation on the banks, including wild banana trees. In the course of our three hour trip we saw monkey, iguana, sloth – two toed and three toed, but we couldn't see their toes; we took Federico's word for it. There were crocodile, small and large, and we thought of Albrecht! However, we were not entirely at ease ourselves when the driver, close to the bank, insisted on teasing a large crocodile from a little distance by heading him off as he went one way and then heading him off again in the opposite direction until he became impatient and dived under the boat and away. We were, to say the least, relieved when he had gone. There were numerous breeds of bird; vulture, great white and little egret, exotic kingfisher and jacana. In parts of Africa the jacana is known as 'the Jesus bird,' from its habit of walking on the leaves of water lilies giving the appearance of walking on water!

On the way up river we stopped at a small police observation station surrounded by the wrecks of boats that had been confiscated because they were found to be carrying drugs or were involved in the illegal trade in green-backed turtle, a rare and preserved species. The police waved us on without inspection; Federico was well connected. A little later we pulled in to a small settlement of only a few houses for the driver to visit his mother who hadn't been well. There were boys swimming in the river, keeping cool and indulging in the universal antics of young boys in water.

Further up the river we met a boat similar to our own, carrying six or eight passengers, that had run out of petrol. Our driver gave him his can of reserve fuel and the other driver met us on the return journey with the replenished can that was essential to get us back.

After the jungle we drove to a small restaurant, Quinbamba, constructed mainly of timber, beside a beach of fine white sand backed by palm trees. There were locals scattered sparsely along the strand that had it been in Europe would have been black with people. We were glad to get in out of the sun and had a lunch of fried plantain with bean sauce and the ubiquitous chips. Hartmut and Hubert had some exotic fish served with head, eyes open, and tail intact.

Oscar then drove us up a hill behind the nearby town of Puerto Limon and pointed out an island in the bay where Christopher Columbus is said to have landed on one of his voyages to the New World. He was looking for water and didn't stay. He named the land Costa Rica - Rich Coast. Oscar then drove us into Puerto Limon which by western standards was a somewhat down-at-heel town with a third world atmosphere. Hartmut bought bananas in a supermarket; an ironic thing to do since *Hornbay* was taking on hundreds of thousands of kilos of them that afternoon. The trouble was, of course, that although Alex had acquired some bananas for his pantry they weren't ripe. Bananas, bananas everywhere and not a one to eat. An endless supply of them was usually available to passengers on these ships from the previous voyage, but since we had come out of dry-dock there were only the unripe bananas we had taken on. Alex produced some a couple of days before we left the ship and they were barely edible. The best bananas consumed on the five week voyage were those that Hartmut bought in a supermarket in Puerto Limon.

Back at the ship we learned that Victor, the third officer, had been too busy to go ashore and would have to wait until he returned to Europe to see a first photograph of his first child. On board we met a new passenger, Marcel. He was German speaking from Zurich, he had been to California to visit his daughter and, averse to long flights, he wanted to return home by sea and had travelled to Moin to join *Horncap*. He was a retired businessman in his sixties, he had a yacht on Lake Zurich, he had good English and he was a great teller of stories. The complement of passengers was now six, so we sat three and three at two tables in the mess, Hartmut joined Hilary and me and Marcel sat with Hubert and Albrecht. Before dinner that evening Alex came into the bar and announced: 'Pilot on board;' we were about to sail. We moved away from the quay and we were set fair for Dover thirteen days away. As it transpired, however, it wasn't just as simple as that.

Next morning before breakfast Hilary and I went up onto the bridge. Boris smiled a broader smile than usual and announced that, after ten hours at sea, we had just altered course. The refrigeration unit was malfunctioning and we were on our way back to Moin! Without efficient refrigeration hundreds of thousands of kilos of fruit would be rotten by the time they arrived at the shops in

Europe. We had no idea how long it would take before we set out again for Dover. There was talk of refrigeration engineers flying out from Europe. Once more passengers were told nothing. If it were to be days before we would sail again, Hilary and I talked about the possibility of leaving the ship for San Jose, the capital, and flying home. That evening back in Moin Alex came into the bar and told us we were moving from the quay to moorings in the harbour and he had no idea how long we would be there. Twenty minutes later he came back into the bar and announced: 'Pilot on board.' We left Moin for the second time having lost a day and a half.

During our day ashore in Costa Rica with the old tar, Hubert, we came to know him better than we had during the outward voyage. He had more English than he was confident to use, and much more than we realised. In fact he was studying English in his cabin. I tentatively offered to help him with an hour's English after breakfast every morning. He jumped at the offer. He was teaching himself in a meticulous, methodical way. He asked me questions about grammar, and the subtleties of the meanings of words that I had to think carefully about and that many a native-born English speaker might not know. I was amazed. What he needed most was to develop his conversation; to have the confidence to use the English he did know. I also discovered that Hubert had a good sense of fun and at our post-breakfast English lessons we laughed a good deal together. One thing in particular gave us great amusement. If some Irish people pronounce 'th' as 'd,' Hubert had similar trouble, but he pronounced 'th' as 'z;' 'zis,' 'zat,' 'zese' and 'zose.'

We were still in the Caribbean. It was hot. Even at night it could be as much as 80 degrees Fahrenheit. It was an awe inspiring experience to stand on deck on a cloudless moonlit night and look at the stars. Being so far south, the only constellation I ever knew how to identify, thanks to Sean O'Casey, was the plough, but it looked different and was in a different place. Some of the other passengers pointed out many stars by name and had a great familiarity with the heavens or perhaps I should say 'sky.'

At sea I was awestruck by the beauty and wonder of the firmament, aware of its unfathomable immensity. It has a greater immediacy in the middle of the ocean than in a city or a suburb. Once more I meditate on this mysterious creation. What's it about? Where do we fit in?

How all this came about is hotly debated between creationists and evolutionists. Creationists believe that the universe was created by God and evolutionists believe that the universe evolved from the Big Bang and is still evolving. Creationists base their belief on the Bible and religious faith and evolutionists base their understanding on scientific knowledge. It isn't, of course, as simple as that. There are churches and religious people today who, because of the incontrovertibility of science, hold that the scientific theory of the origin of the universe, the Big Bang, does not preclude the belief that it was created by God; that this was God's way of doing it.

Stephen Hawking, the Cambridge astrophysicist, has recounted that at an astronomy conference in the Vatican the Pope said they should not research into the beginning of the universe itself because that was the work of God. It was, however, okay with the Pope to study the universe after it began. Hawking went on to say that he was glad he hadn't heard his paper earlier in the conference on how the universe began as he didn't relish the thought of being handed over to the Inquisition like Galileo!

For the Pope the ultimate authority in these matters is theology, while the ultimate authority for Hawking is science. Throughout history the Church claimed to be the final arbiter in all such matters, but since the 17th century it has slowly had to accommodate to science on many issues. It wasn't, however, until 1992 that the Church finally absolved Galileo, who had been condemned by the Inquisition in the 16th century for his belief that the earth went round the sun rather than, that which the Church taught, based on the Bible, that the sun went round the earth.

Amongst Christians today there are those who hold every conceivable view in the theology/science debate. At one end of the spectrum fundamentalist Christians, and they exist in every Christian tradition, believe that the issue of the origin of the universe is a simple matter. The Bible, in the book of Genesis, gives an account of creation by God and since they believe that the Bible is infallible, and is to be taken literally, that's how the whole thing started and that's the end of the matter. At the other end of the spectrum there are theologians who claim that on this and on many other topics they can marry theology and science and remain true to both.

Many people don't take an interest in these matters. They simply want to get on with their lives, doing whatever it is that they are doing. Only a small number of people are reflective when it comes to theological issues. People who are interested and do want to think about creation and religion often find themselves swayed one way or another by reading or listening to people they consider well-informed or authoritative on the topics. The pattern often is that they listen to one side of the argument and find it has merit and then listen to the opposite side of the argument and find it has merit. Constantly listening to others, especially those who clearly have more knowledge on the topics than oneself, can make it very difficult to come to a conclusion.

Over the years I read a great deal about theological controversies and finally decided that I would make up my own mind rather than look any further for answers from the opinions of others, no matter how authoritative and well-informed they appeared to be. The position I finally came to was that the scientific analysis was credible and that theological analyses, of whatever hue, were not. This led me further than simply deciding on the matter of creation. It led me to the conclusion that there was no God, no revelation, no divinity of Jesus, no miraculous intervention in the world, no life after death and no Second Coming. For someone who spent the best part of 40 years involved in Christian ministry you may think that this must have been traumatic for me. On the contrary it gave me great freedom and peace. It was a long slow process, but when I finally decided that I could no longer believe, it came to me as a great relief.

We are all in danger of submitting ourselves to the institutions to which we belong. We are in danger of subverting something of our potential to grow and develop as people to the objectives of the institution. Membership of institutions is often not conducive to our own emotional development; rather institutions require loyalty to their doctrine, philosophy or objectives at the expense of the personal freedom that allows us to grow as people. This is true not only of the institutional Church, but it is true of political parties, trade unions and of all institutions. It is in the nature of an institution that its own wellbeing and survival come before the wellbeing, and often at the expense, of its individual members. We make all the important decisions of our lives with our emotions, and emotions are at the bottom of the list of priorities of institutions if they are there at all.

For some people membership of the Church is the security of belonging to the group. For some it fills the need to have other people to do their thinking for them. For some it provides identity. The liturgy of the Church can be a great comfort in a precarious and fast changing world in which there is much evil. The Church is based on theological doctrines that were formulated in a pre-scientific world when it was not uncommon for notable human beings to be thought to be divine, and where the existence of angels, demons and miraculous events were taken for granted.

These doctrines and teachings don't stand up after the best part of two millennia of the evolution of the thinking and experience of humankind.

After I had finally made up my own mind I still thought from time to time about some churchmen and theologians of stature who obviously still believed. They were finer minds than mine and many of them had much more theology than I had. It didn't give me serious doubts about my own conclusions, but I wondered. I wondered how they could believe so many things that I found incredible. I reminded myself that I had believed some of these things for most of my life. I adjusted that thought, however, to: I had accepted some of these things for most of my life. I had accepted them on trust from 2,000 years of the teaching and tradition of the Church and I had got on with my work with people in the ministry, which I enjoyed. When I finally realised that nobody could give me answers I made up my own mind. I can imagine somebody saying: 'Who are you to disagree with the wisdom of ages, the great minds of the Church over two millennia?' Over the years since I have been reassured to come across quotations from some significant philosophical and literary figures who advocated such independence of thought. Immanuel Kant in his essay 'What Is Enlightenment?' says:

Enlightenment is man's emergence from his self-imposed immaturity. Immaturity is the inability to use one's understanding without guidance from another. This immaturity is self- imposed when its cause lies not in lack of understanding, but in lack of resolve and courage to use it without guidance from another. Have courage to use your own understanding.'

William Hazlitt in his essay 'On the Ignorance of the Learned' says:

'You might as well ask the paralytic to leap from his chair, and throw away his crutch, or, without a miracle, to "take up his bed and walk," as expect the learned reader to throw down his book and think for himself.'

Walt Whitman in his poem 'Song of Myself' says:

'You shall no longer take things at second or third
hand, nor look through the eyes of the dead,
nor feed on the spectres in books,
You shall not look through my eyes either, nor take
things from me,
You shall listen to all sides and filter them from yourself.'

The librettist W.S.Gilbert makes the same point in a more humorous way. In the Gilbert and Sullivan operetta 'HMS Pinafore' Sir Joseph Porter sings:

I grew so rich that I was sent
By a pocket borough into Parliament.
I always voted at my party's call,
And I never thought of thinking for myself at all.
I thought so little, they rewarded me
By making me the Ruler of the Queen's Navee!

All these quotations are saying the same thing: make up your own mind. Hazlitt and Whitman say explicitly: stop looking for it in books; it is in yourself that you look. Inform yourself and filter things from yourself. However, Gilbert is making the point that not thinking for yourself will help you to get on in the world.

I don't feel the need for others, humble or exalted, to believe what I do. I am perfectly comfortable that where I am is right for me and I don't feel the need to convince anyone else to agree with me. I believe, however, that what I now hold makes some other people uncomfortable. One friend has told another friend that I should not publish my views; I should keep them to myself. Another good friend, a priest, was careful to tell me that Anthony Flew, the philosopher, a long time atheist now believes in God again. The implication that I took from what he said was: 'if a man as eminent in philosophy as Flew has changed his mind, maybe you will too.' Maybe I will or maybe I won't. I discovered however that Flew while affirming his belief in God says he does not believe in special revelation. It looks to me that he holds a position akin to the 18th century Deists. He says explicitly: 'I still hope and believe there's no possibility of an afterlife.' Yet another friend, a clergyman, told me that Alister McGrath, a former science professor turned theologian, had answered the arguments of Richard Dawkins, the atheist geneticist. In these instances I should have said: 'Don't mind Flew, don't mind Mc Grath, what do you think?' I didn't, but I will the next time. It is human for us to want other people to agree with us, especially people considered authorities, but it is unwise to abdicate to them, no matter how learned or authoritative, decisions on matters that are within our own competence to decide. People who swallowed Marx and Freud hook, line and sinker nowadays have reason to believe that they should have been a little more discerning!

The truth of the matter is that most people, religious and non-religious, do not reflect on these matters at all. Religious people accept the Church's position on creation and many other things, on trust, because the Church teaches them; and if they have doubts they don't voice them because they find the practice of their religion comforting, a support in life, and don't want to risk losing it. On controversial issues religious people sometimes say: 'I don't want to go there.' Many people who do not practise religion don't reflect on these matters either; they are too busy getting on with life and these matters are not important to them. Some people do, however, make up their minds, but are not interested enough to discuss it with others. In Ireland, in what has been a religion obsessed society until recently, to have declared oneself an atheist was to be a pariah, perhaps to invoke pity as much as condemnation. Today this is less and less the case.

I believe, however, that many people, including clergy, have serious doubts but they don't pursue them. Four or five years ago I told one clergyman I had not seen since student days, lest there were crossed lines between us, that I no longer believed some of the essential doctrines of the Christian faith. His response was: 'Join the gang.' He was still active in the parochial ministry.

When we look at the sky and try to comprehend its size and its age, as told to us by the astrophysicists, the question arises as to why a God would create a universe of such unfathomable immensity in order to work through his scheme of salvation. Why would he want to create the vastness of the universe and use for his purposes, relatively speaking, only the speck of a speck of it, namely, our world. If there is life similar to our own somewhere else in the universe, the question arises whether God has had an incarnation there. Or perhaps the beings on such a planet will have behaved themselves and won't have needed a divine incarnation and a system of atonement.

The rest of our solar system appears to have no bearing on a divine plan of salvation.

Would something a little more modest than the size of the universe not have done?

What do we say about the complexity of the micro-world as we know it from the insights of quantum mechanics? Was there not a simpler way to create a testing ground for humans? Why create a system where it is necessary for humans to kill animals, and animals to kill other animals in order to survive? How can an all-loving all-powerful God allow suffering on the scale that we see as we look around the world, for human beings, and for animals for that matter? Much of this suffering is innocent in that the individual enduring the suffering has done nothing to cause it. The answer some religious people give to this problem is to say that God has created humankind with free will and all of these things are traceable to somebody back along the line having exercised their free will to make sinful decisions that cause suffering in succeeding generations. Is it fair for a God to allow little babies to be born with cancer because some ancestor did something wrong? The suffering and pain and death that earthquakes, tornados and tsunamis cause to hundreds of thousands of people cannot be attributed to human sinfulness. How could an all-merciful, all-loving, all-powerful God stand by and do nothing in the face of all the evils of the world, even if some of them are the result of human action? These, and many others, are the questions that bedevilled me in the past. When God is removed from the equation, the Big Bang, evolution and the insights of science answer these questions. I find the scientific account of the universe credible. I find accounts that include God in one way or another not credible.

However the universe came to be and for whatever reason, if any, it fills one with reverential awe to contemplate on a clear night from the deck of a ship at sea the immensity of the starry sky, knowing that it contains as many galaxies as there are grains of sand on every beach and desert in the world. To know that it stretches outwards for billions and billions of miles and has existed for over 14 billion years is to be overcome by the mystery of it all and to feel one's own insignificance, and the insignificance of all humankind. In the unfathomable immensity of it many people believe that we, on earth, are the only form of life, as we understand it, in the universe. Some scientists, however, believe that there may well be life somewhere out there. Why do we on earth have the right balance of conditions that have allowed life to develop? Either a creator God somehow arranged it so, or these conditions came about purely by chance.

Looking at human life itself there is no theme, dimension or underlying structure of any kind that points to life having a meaning. The dynamic that does underlie and motivates all life is the vitality for life itself in all its forms, human, animal and plant; the powerful life-force in all living things that ensures procreation and the survival of species. Within this universal force there is competition for survival from viruses and bugs that threaten human life. All of this great complexity must be coped with as an integral part of living, but it gives no hint as to a meaning or purpose for life itself.

This is where religion comes in. Human beings developed rituals and modes of behaviour in order to keep favour with the supernatural divine powers that they perceived to be the source of their food and other necessities for survival and to protect them from all that might threaten them. When the sun shone and the rain came they believed that their god was pleased with them and their crops prospered so they performed a ritual to thank him. When there was thunder and lightning they perceived that he was angry and punishing them so they performed a ritual to appease him. When they defeated another marauding tribe they performed another ritual to thank their god for victory.

Nothing changes. These days Churches have services of thanksgiving to God for giving them the harvest. They do this despite the fact that millions of people throughout the world die of starvation every year as a result of drought, and God doesn't appear to do anything to help them to survive. When Aids emerged as a universal disease some churchmen and religious people said it was a punishment from God for the practice of homosexuality, which was the same reason some people said God punished the people of Lisbon with the earthquake on All Saints Day 1755. When Britain won the Falklands war the Church of England put on a service of thanksgiving for the defeat of Argentina which the Royal Family and members of the British government attended. Religious people invoke God in the most incongruous ways.

While the gurus of religion still proclaim the involvement of God in the world, people get on with their lives under the imperative of nature. They are born, grow to maturity, procreate and die and the cycle goes on. During the space of a lifetime some people, in order to avoid the existential nausea, the experience of meaninglessness, involve themselves in the meaning that religion purports to give, all the while filling their time with the occupations necessary to survive. Some people go further and give themselves purpose by accumulating wealth, excelling at sport, positing alternative religions and a million other ways, including going on cargo ship voyages, to occupy themselves until they come to die.

As I said earlier, out on the ocean we were away from the obsession with news that ashore is pumped at us by the media all day every day. News that brings into our homes the pain and suffering of the world with accounts of wars, starvation, murder, rape, drugs, gangland crime, inter-personal bitterness, hatred and many more unthinkable human activities. Listening to and reading about all these unspeakable travesties of human decency every day cannot be good for us. As we know it is only rarely that the media report the good things that people do; the often heroic care of people by people; the love for each other that does give some meaning to life. Such love and care are the ethical and moral virtues of religion without the miraculous and without aspirations for religious salvation. Despite what some religious people say it is possible to have one without the other. It is possible to live a meaningful moral life without the metaphysical assumptions of religion. It is possible to live lives where the purpose is to be loving and caring for other people, to create a decent society without the necessity of believing in miracles, resurrections, divine intervention, and life after death. It is possible because many atheists, humanists, agnostics and unselfconsciously non-religious people do it all the time.

CHAPTER 7

H aving left Moin for the second time we sailed north east across the Caribbean. We had passed Jamaica, through the Windward Passage between Cuba and Haiti, then through the Mouchoir Passage east of the Turks and Caicos Islands; we were a day's sailing out of the Caribbean into the Atlantic. We had just returned from lunch to our cabin to collect our books to go to the shaded spot on deck to sit and read and probably snooze in the warmth of the early afternoon sun, when the bell outside our cabin door sounded seven times followed by a single ring, and then was continuous.

'That's muster stations,' Hilary said, who had listened more carefully than I had when we were instructed on safety procedures on the outward voyage.

'Take your time,' I said, 'it's just a drill.' Hilary opened the cabin door. There was a strong acrid smell of smoke, like burning paint, outside. We grabbed our life-jackets and wet suits and made for our muster station. Had we been on deck when the alarm went, not having been told otherwise, we would have gone down to our cabins to collect life-jackets and wet suits. The correct safety procedure is that there should be a supply of life-jackets at muster stations and passengers elsewhere on board than in cabins should go straight there. We learned later that many passengers, who were on deck on the Lusitania when she was hit by a torpedo, lost their lives because they returned to their cabins to collect their life-jackets.

Hilary went first. Along the alleyway the thought came to me that everything I had left behind in the cabin I could happily abandon except one item. It was all easily replaceable except the work I had done on my laptop. I remembered my computer backup stick, turned around and went back to the cabin. I found it and set out again. On the stairs there were crew members rushing in all directions. Hilary realised that I wasn't behind her. She shouted. I didn't hear. She pushed her way back and found me on my way.

'That was a stupid thing to do,' she said. I knew she was right, so I didn't respond. We saw Oleg, the ship's cook, with life-jacket, wet suit and hard hat on the way to his muster station. Passing the second deck alleyway there was smoke. When we arrived on deck at our muster station Alex, in boiler suit and hard hat, Hartmut and Marcel were already there. 'Fire in machine,' Alex told us and he left quickly to find Hubert and Albrecht. When he came back he pointed out the lifeboat that passengers would use. We waited. As the only woman on board, Hilary would be first into the lifeboat. The Captain, however, wouldn't be there too! He'd have to wait until last and there was another lifeboat for him that Alex also pointed out. As we stood there not knowing what to expect I had a mental picture of emerging from the arrivals door of an airport somewhere, facing the world's press and giving an account of how having abandoned ship, we watched the burned out hull of *Horncap* disappear beneath the waves. How we were buffeted around like corks on the ocean until we were finally rescued dramatically by a ship that had picked up our SOS signal.

No marks for realising that nothing like this happened. After about half an hour Alex on his walkie talkie got the 'all clear.' They had extinguished the fire. No drama, no lifeboats, no burned out hull, no airport, no heroics. We trooped back to our cabins, replaced our life-jackets and wet suits, collected our books and went up on deck to read. Marcel thought it had all been an exercise, but it hadn't, it had been the real thing, and if they had not been able to bring the fire under control some of the fantasy might have become reality.

The sea had been relatively smooth, but that night it changed. We were in the worst weather we had on the voyage; the ship was rolling and pitching badly, there were waves 20 or 30 feet high, our speed was down from 19 to 10 or 11 knots. When some powerful waves hit the ship it shuddered and felt like it would stop. Lashing rain made for poor visibility. It was certainly gale force 8, and possibly storm force 9. The rain battered the windows of the bridge. Virtually every dip of the bow into a trough sent spray over the containers on deck and as far back as the windows of the wheelhouse, which would have become opaque with salt but for the rain and the use of wipers with fresh water spray, just like a car. We had to be very careful moving about our cabin not to be thrown around. Doing anything was hazardous. Putting toothpaste on my toothbrush I ended up in a heap in the shower. It was undoubtedly the heaviest weather we had had. If we had had to attend muster stations that night we would have been very frightened indeed and if we had had to abandon ship I cannot see how we could have survived. I was reminded of a ship I boarded when working in Rotterdam that had berthed having recently come through a severe storm. The sea had stripped paint off the hull, the deck was littered with items that should have been stowed or tied down and I met an abstracted seaman emerging from the stairway to the galley eating from his hand a soft fried egg.

The following day I met the Captain on the bridge. He was sitting on the high chair in front of the instruments. The first time I had seen an officer on the bridge sitting. He was weary and unshaven. I greeted him and he said: 'Trouble with ship, trouble with cargo, trouble with engine; going to Azores.' In fact I already knew this as earlier in the day Boris, the second officer, told me we had altered course and we were heading for Ponte Delgada because the refrigeration system had finally failed and the Azores was the nearest landfall. Without refrigeration the cargo of fruit was seriously at risk. He had asked me not to say anything until we were told.

In the mess, shortly after I had been talking to the Captain, Alex breezed in and announced that we were going to the Azores; he would be arranging for passengers a tour of the island on which we landed, we would stay a night in a hotel and the company would fly us home the following day. This would be some compensation for ending our voyage a few days early, but Hilary and I would be sorry to miss staying with Derek and Jenny in Dover as planned, and giving them an account of our adventure.

On the voyage, but especially when things went wrong, I was constantly reminded that in this era of globalisation and when it is possible to travel half way round the world in 24 hours, transporting the humble banana from the producer in the West Indies and Central America to the consumer in Europe was, in contrast, a slow laborious process. This one shipping line alone had ships arriving in Europe every week carrying hundreds of thousands of kilos of bananas and other fruits, and there were other shipping lines doing something similar. We all knew we would never look at a banana in quite the same way again. Nor would we think of the sea in quite the same way again; its immensity, its disinterest in whoever is bold to cross it, its beauty, its moods, above all its anger, its hidden life and its place in the scheme of things.

The story of men's lives on the great seas and oceans of the world is recorded in literature from the very beginning. There is a beautiful passage in Psalm 107, written sometime in the millennium before Christ, at a time when God was believed to control nature like a puppeteer and to manipulate it for his purposes. Today, with the insights of science, we understand things differently. None the less the passage is worth quoting for its imagery and the beauty of the language:

'Those that go down to the sea in ships and occupy their business in great waters; these men see the works of the Lord and his wonders in the deep. For at his word the stormy wind arises which lifts up the waves thereof. They are carried up to the heaven, and down again to the deep, their soul melts away because of the trouble. They reel to and fro and stagger like a drunken man and are at their wits end. So when they cry unto the Lord in their trouble he delivers them out of their distress. For he makes the storm to cease so that the waves thereof are still. Then are they glad because they are at rest and so he brings them unto the haven where they would be.'

In his poem 'Sea Fever,' John Masefield has a rather more romantic view of the sea:

'I must go down to the seas again, to the lonely sea and the sky,/ and all I ask is a tall ship and a star to steer her by,.........'

Literature is peppered with stories of the lives of people at sea: in English, most notably in the works of Joseph Conrad, himself a mariner, whose first language was Polish but who wrote the finest of literary English. William Golding, who had a lifelong obsession with ships and the sea, set his 'Sea Trilogy' on the voyage of a sailing ship between England and Australia.

On our voyage on *Hornbay* there was yet one more surprise event, but this time it was a pleasant one. I had secured Hilary's agreement not to reveal that my birthday occurred while we were at sea. At breakfast that morning, to my amazement, Alex emerged from the galley carrying aloft a large birthday cake, holding a bottle of 'Krim,' Crimean champagne, and with a Horn Line umbrella over his arm. I looked to Hilary who though highly amused protested: 'I didn't.' All present launched into 'Happy birthday to you....' which I found embarrassing beyond endurance. Alex had noted my date of birth on his passenger list and being the good chief steward that he was he marked it. The cake, a Black Forest gateau, was to be kept until tea in the afternoon and Alex presented me with the umbrella and the champagne.

We were a day or so out from Ponte Delgada and that evening there was one more event laid on for passengers; a farewell dinner. I may be wrong, but I suspect it was provided to compensate passengers for all the things that had gone wrong, whether on the initiative of Alex, the Captain or Head Office in Hamburg I wouldn't know. There was a special menu with wine on the house, or rather, on the ship. It was no doubt a pain in the neck for Oleg and Dymi to produce something different again. Half the complement of the two officers who attended was sober. The whole affair was a damp squib, but in the bar afterwards the evening picked up again with the cutting of the birthday cake and another bottle of red Crimean Champagne.

Before we arrived at Ponte Delgada, which was estimated to be early evening, passengers received an e-mail from Hamburg to say we would spend the night on board and leave the ship at 7.30 am in the morning to catch flights home. We were glad enough to be going home, since we would not have relished staying on board for however long it would take to fix what was wrong with the refrigeration unit and the ship. There would be no hotel or tour of the island as Alex had told us. The flights had already been booked.

We were simply informed of the decision peremptorily made by Horn Line. Hilary and I, given the option, would certainly have stayed a night or two at our own expense to look around the island. Hartmut, on behalf of the passengers, spoke to Hamburg on the ship's phone to register our disapproval at the abrupt way things had been organised and to try to make a new arrangement. Head Office told him that the flights had been booked and there would be no change. I was with Hartmut, but as he spoke in German I didn't know what he said, but from his tone of voice I knew that he left the woman at the other end in no doubt that the passengers were not pleased.

We docked at around 7.00 pm and two members of the company's agents came on board. One of these was Scottish, and when he saw me waiting to speak to Alex he came over and asked me if anybody from Horn Line had apologised to us that our voyage had been cut short. When I told him how things had been he was incensed and said that insofar as he represented the company he apologised. At my request he gave me the name and e-mail address of the managing director. During this conversation who was skulking near the door? You've guessed; the bold Seven Thirty indulging his addiction to eavesdropping.

Hilary and I were determined to go ashore, have a good meal and a look around Ponte Delgada. The agent recommended a restaurant, Alex ordered a taxi and Marcel came with us. The other three stayed on board. We found the restaurant, which turned out to be a catering school, and we had an excellent, relaxed meal served perfectly by two beautiful, smiling and helpful waitresses; a greater contrast to Seven Thirty one could not imagine. When our taxi arrived to take us back to the ship we asked the driver to bring us on a tour of the town. For half an hour he drove us along main streets and up and down narrow back streets in the old district. He pointed out significant buildings and places of interest. Ponte Delgada is a fine city where the old and the new have been blended together well. In the old part we saw something that none of us had ever seen before; long stretches of footpath surfaced with patterns of black and white mosaics. We learned later that this was a feature on the Portuguese mainland too and can be seen in the old parts of Lisbon and other Portuguese cities. The black mosaic pieces are from the volcanic rock of the Azores and the white come from the mainland. The Azores have the distinction of being the only place in Europe where tea is grown. The islands are all of volcanic origin. The Azoreans say that in the 15th century the British claimed one of the islands, raised their flag on it and went away. When they returned the island had disappeared and I have no doubt that the Brits blamed the Portuguese!

Next morning two taxis arrived at the ship at 7.30 am and took us to the airport. We flew to Lisbon. There we said goodbye to our shipmates, Hartmut, Hubert, Albrecht and Marcel. We flew to Heathrow and on to Dublin.

CHAPTER 8

The most frequently asked question by our friends was: 'Would you do it again?' For both of us the answer was an unequivocal 'yes'. We enjoyed the voyage; it was a great experience despite some frustrations. In fact in many ways the hitches added to the adventure. If everything had gone swimmingly, metaphorically speaking, it might not have been so interesting. Towards the end of the voyage we asked Boris if in his 30 or more years at sea he had ever been on a voyage where so many things had gone wrong. He laughed and shook his head, 'Never.'

We decided that we would go on a cargo ship voyage again but next time we will probably go south into the Mediterranean or perhaps north to the Baltic and will hope to make more ports of call where we can go ashore. One possibility is to voyage to St Petersburg, stay for a few days and either return by cargo vessel or by train, for we enjoy train travel too. Next time we would ensure that we travelled with a Western European crew, preferably English speaking. It was an experience sailing with Ukrainians and Latvians, but their reluctance to communicate and difficulty in doing so when they decided to, was a problem. The Captain, to whom all e-mails to the ship from Head office were sent, did not always pass on those addressed to us. He had never sailed with passengers before and at one stage he said that there should not have been passengers on the voyage. He didn't say it unpleasantly, but meant that there was the possibility of something problematic about a ship on its first voyage after dry dock. It's just like a car. It's going well when you leave it into the garage for a service and often gives trouble when it comes back. The newly fitted refrigeration unit seemed to have given trouble from the start before it finally gave up. I have no doubt that the chief officer and Seven Thirty would certainly have preferred if there had not been passengers.

While the voyage was all still fresh in my mind I wrote to the managing director of Horn Line in the following terms:

I recounted to him the difficulty the crew seemed to have communicating with passengers. What caused this, I was not sure. It may have been crew not familiar with having passengers on board, lack of confidence in the language or reticence arising from a different cultural background. I also registered the disappointment of passengers at the peremptory way in which they were told that the voyage had been cut short. Passengers understood the reason for the ending of the voyage at the Azores and the difficulty this created for the shipping line, but they would like to have been told in a more sympathetic way.

I had in reply a most conciliatory letter. Herr Bevensee apologised without reservation, said that in future they would take account of these issues when dealing with the agency from which they employed crew. He also refunded to us and to all the passengers 10 per cent of our fare. This was not my reason for writing. In many ways all the unscheduled events made it a more interesting trip, but the voyage would have been much enhanced had the crew been at least friendly.

I learned subsequently that some of the other passengers had written to Horn Line too giving their views, and received a similar reply, including notification of 10% fare refund. I replied thanking Herr Bevensee for his reasonable and contrite e-mail. He replied reiterating his apology and his thanks to me for taking the trouble to write.

I would have been curious to know what happened to the ship; the engine, refrigeration unit and the cargo of fruit, but I didn't feel I could ask.

THE MEDITERRANEAN

Second Voyage: Southampton, through the Strait of Gibraltar into the Mediterranean to first port of call, Salerno (Italy). Then to Piraeus (Greece), Izmir (Turkey), Alexandria (Egypt), Limassol (Cyprus), Ashdod (Israel), and on the way back Salerno again, Savona (Italy), Setubal (Portugal) and Portbury which is the port of Bristol.

INTRODUCTION

Insurance companies used to call it an 'Act of God.' Claims for loss resulting from an act of God are excluded from insurance policies. Companies don't go on to say that any such claims should be referred to the Church, but maybe it would be worth a try! This is the theme of the Billy Connolly film 'The Man Who Sued God'. I am thinking of course of the recent volcanic eruption in Iceland that created havoc with air travel in Europe.

Earthquakes are also acts of God. If there is a God it is just conceivable that he or she might cause a volcano to erupt to remind humankind that we are not as in control of this mysterious and wonderful world as we take for granted; that our hold on civilisation is much more precarious than we think. On the other hand I cannot begin to comprehend what kind of God would cause or even allow an earthquake that kills hundreds of thousands of people, men, women and innocent children. If there is a God that presides over this kind of thing it is hard to escape the conclusion that he is malevolent. If it is understood as simply a vagary of the natural order it falls into place and as such it is perfectly credible. That there is a God that has anything to do with earthquakes doesn't make any sense. All the difficulties caused by calling these kinds of events acts of God are solved if we call them something like 'Functions of Nature.' Maybe this is what insurance companies should have called them.

All of this is a prelude to telling you that at the time of the volcanic eruption in Iceland it took Hilary and me five days to travel home overland from Munich to Dublin. We had turned up at Munich airport for our flight, in the expectation of being in Dublin in a few hours, to be told along with hundreds of other passengers that the airport was closed and all flights had been cancelled because of the eruption in Iceland. In passing, and not pertinent to the story I am about to tell, I would like to record that despite the fact that my travel policy did not cover acts of God, the insurance company did pay my claim for the extra travel expense and accommodation necessary for our five day surface journey home. What a kind insurance company!

What happened was that as soon as we arrived from the airport at our hotel back in Munich I phoned home to our insurance broker and asked him if we were covered by our travel insurance. He said he would phone the company and call me back. In about half an hour he phoned to say that he had spoken to our insurers and they confirmed that we were covered. After we arrived home our broker told us that about two hours after the company had confirmed to him that we were covered he received a notice to say that loss consequential upon the Iceland volcano eruption was not covered under their travel policies. In the circumstances our broker told us to submit our claim, which we did and, true to its word, the company paid it. It seems that contrary to popular opinion insurance companies are, after all, honourable, decent and generous institutions!

Two weeks after our return from Munich we were due to sail on a cargo ship from Southampton on a four week voyage in the Mediterranean, secure in the knowledge that even if the volcano were still spewing out its infernal debris, it would not interfere with marine navigation. However in order to join our ship we had already booked a flight from Dublin to Gatwick to connect with a train to Southampton. As I have already mentioned one of the immutable rules of cargo ship voyaging is that a vessel will not wait for passengers who are late. If you aren't there when the ship is ready to sail she will go without you. We weren't prepared to take the risk that there might be more volcanic dust around that might cause our flight to be delayed or cancelled so we forfeited our air fare and booked onto the ferry from Dublin Port to Holyhead.

It is interesting to reflect that the exact opposite happened to our plans for our West Indies cargo ship voyage, when to join our ship at Dover we had booked to travel by ferry from Dun Laoghaire to Holyhead and by train to Dover. On that occasion on the days before we were due to cross there were more acts of God; storms in the Irish Sea that caused some ferry crossings to be cancelled. Unwilling to take the risk that our crossing might be delayed or cancelled we abandoned our plans to travel by ferry and booked a flight from Dublin to Heathrow and travelled to Dover by train. It is perfectly possible that if two acts of God, storms in the Irish Sea and a volcanic eruption in Iceland, occurred at the same time such Divine inconsiderateness would mean that our cargo ship would sail without us.

When we tell people that we are going on a cargo ship voyage, the comment that is most often made is something to the effect, 'I didn't know you could travel on cargo ships. Do you know somebody or how do you get to do that?' Our answer: 'You can travel almost anywhere in the world on cargo ships; you can even circumnavigate the world if you have time; it takes about six months.'

It's just a matter of finding one of a number of travel agents that specialise in arranging passage on cargo vessels. As we have seen, on a cargo ship the cargo has priority. Passengers are secondary to commercial considerations except if the ship is about to sink, when passengers will take precedence over cargo! Under normal circumstances the only time that the precedence of cargo comes into play is in port when the time taken to load or discharge freight determines the length of time passengers will have to go ashore. In these days when quick turn around in port is important for economic reasons, passengers can usually go ashore for anything between a couple of hours and the best part of a day. Because of the short time of loading or discharging or for reasons of security in a port, occasionally passengers cannot go ashore at all. This was the case once out of nine ports on this voyage and one out of eight ports on our previous voyage.

When joining a ship it is essential that the night before embarkation passengers stay close enough to the port in case departure time is changed. The ship's agent keeps in touch with passengers by telephone in case the ship is to sail earlier or later than scheduled. On this voyage we stayed with a cousin of mine in Winchester, half an hour from Southampton, and arrived at the quay to board *Gran Bretagna* at the appointed time.

CHAPTER 1

We knew she would be a bigger ship than the one we had travelled on 18 months previously to the West Indies, but we didn't realise how big; she was huge. She was a roll-on-roll-off car carrier that held over two and a half thousand new cars on her 11 decks. She also took on and discharged a small number of lorry tractors, JCBs, bulldozers and other commercial vehicles, some containers and other bits and pieces. When in port everything, cargo, passengers and crew, boarded and left the ship by the ramp that was lowered onto the quay from the stern of the ship. The line was Italian, Grimaldi, one of the biggest shipping lines in Europe, and for those who know about these things she was built 1998/1999, her gross tonnage was 51,700, she was 181 metres in length and her beam was 32.25 metres. Her maximum speed was 20 knots and she had a crew of 26.

Our taxi dropped us to the quay and Stelio greeted us at the top of the ramp. He introduced himself as the chief officer. He was wearing overalls and a reflective jacket as he supervised the discharge of cargo. He took our passports and called an able seaman who carried our cases and brought us by lift to the top deck. The steward arrived and took us to our cabin. We had booked what is known as the 'owner's cabin,' which is the best of the cabins available to passengers. On this ship four of the other five passenger cabins are inboard and didn't have a view of the sea. Not only does the owner's cabin have a sea view, but it is spacious and better equipped than the others. It had a double bed rather than twin bunks and a bathroom including bath and shower. It had a sitting room with sofa, chairs and a desk.

We soon learned that we would be the only passengers on this voyage. Now the matter of other passengers on a cargo ship voyage can be a plus or a minus. Fellow voyagers can be interesting and stimulating to be with or they can be boring, irritating, annoying and talk too much. However if they are not the best of company it is not difficult to get away from them and make your own space.

Our itinerary was: Southampton, through the Strait of Gibraltar into the Mediterranean to our first port of call, Salerno (Italy). Then to Piraeus (Greece), Izmir (Turkey), Alexandria (Egypt), Limassol (Cyprus), Ashdod (Israel), and on the way back Salerno again, Savona (Italy), Setubal (Portugal) and Portbury which is the port of Bristol where we would disembark. This takes four weeks. The ship continues to Cork (Ireland), Esbjerg (Denmark), Wallhamn (Sweden), Antwerp (Belgium) and back to Southampton. The full round voyage takes six weeks.

We unpacked, settled in and went for a walk around the deck, where there were hundreds of new cars, each one strapped from wheel hubs to rings on the deck. We found our bearings; our cabin was on the deck below the bridge. We bumped into the Captain, a man in his late forties from Sorrento. He was friendly and ready for a chat. We went back to our cabin and were sitting reading when there was a knock on the door. It was the steward, sent by the Captain to tell us that a huge cruise liner, Grand Princess, was about to leave harbour and we might like to see it from the bridge. She had berthed early in the morning and in twelve hours she had disgorged 3,000 passengers, had taken on another 3,000 and was off for a two week cruise, first stop Malaga. It was quite a sight. We commented that we would not be interested in such a cruise preferring a cargo ship. The Captain said he would love the luxury of one of these cruises as for him *Gran Bretagna* meant work.

When dinner time came we found our way to the officers' mess where we sat at the passengers' table. Across from us there was a junior officers' table with three young engineers and two young deck officers. With the exception of one second mate who was a Filipino, all the ship's officers, deck and engineer, were Italian.

Each day aboard was to be punctuated by a simple continental breakfast and a cooked lunch and dinner. The cook was Lanzo who did an excellent job in catering to our vegetarian needs. He would put his head around the door of the mess from time to time to make sure everything was all right. The steward, who served meals, was another Lanzo. In height and build, and particularly in his accent when speaking English, he was a dead ringer for Manuel from Barcelona, the waiter in *Fawlty Towers*. Lanzo the steward was from Avalino, a small town in the hinterland of Salerno. One day we were a little late going to the mess for dinner. There was a knock on our cabin door and there he stood. He smiled, pointed down the alleyway towards the mess and said 'Ees ready.' It could have been Manuel.

After dinner on that first evening we went up to the bridge which is not only the hub of the ship from where everything is controlled, it is the place from where the best view all round is to be had. Before going onto the bridge in the first place it is important that passengers ask the Captain for permission. Ninety nine Captains out of a hundred give permission willingly. There is, however, a certain sensitivity needed on the part of passengers on cargo ships when they are on the bridge. They should not speak to officers on duty when they are plotting on charts, reading instruments or when they are otherwise occupied. When the pilot is on board they should stay at one end of the bridge away from crew and instruments and especially when the ship is berthing. Should there be an emergency of any kind passengers should leave the bridge. Most of the time, especially at sea, it is perfectly acceptable for passengers to be on the bridge and officers on watch can be glad to chat with them when they are not busy. It is the place from where you can see sea life around you and, with binoculars, depending upon where the ship is, you can see perhaps whales, dolphins, flying fish and birds and of course other ships.

On that first night leaving Southampton when we arrived onto the bridge it was in darkness except for the light from the navigation screens. The Captain and pilot were there. The pilot spoke to us warmly and asked if we were English. We said we were

Irish and in a very English accent he told us that his father was from Galway and his own name was Seán O'Toole. He laughed at the incongruity. We stood quietly at one end of the bridge while *Gran Bretagna* eased away from the quay and moved slowly down the Solent in response to the directions of Seán O'Toole. Between his instructions to the AB, the able seaman, at the helm the pilot talked to us about modern electronic technology and up-to-date satellite aids to navigation and said: 'and still ships are bumping into each other all over the place.' When we were into open water Seán O'Toole said goodbye and left the bridge to board his launch which was hovering alongside to take him ashore.

As we stood there in the dark the AB came over to us and asked if we would like coffee. Despite not being seasoned coffee drinkers, we said 'yes,' and he came back in a few minutes with two small disposable plastic cups of very sweet extra strong espresso coffee like warm liqueur. It was delicious. These strong shots of espresso coffee were to become a feature of our time on the bridge for the rest of the voyage.

Next morning before breakfast, as was our wont on previous voyages, we went up to the bridge to read the co-ordinates to see how far on we were after the night's sailing. There the Captain regaled us with stories of his life at sea. He was a tall, well built, good looking man with black bushy hair with no discernable parting. He had a broad forehead and brown eyes and his face narrowed towards a strong chin. His complexion was sallow. One had no difficulty believing that he was Italian. He was, he told us, fifty. He had developed a larger stomach than was proportionate to his build. He walked with not quite a swagger, but with the confidence of a man in charge who knew what he was about. He talked at the top of his voice, and when he became excited, as he did when talking about Napoli, the football team he supported with schoolboy enthusiasm, he added emphasis to what he was saying with extravagant gestures; hands and arms waving in all directions. When he was performing as Captain, especially coming into or leaving port, even to one who didn't speak his language, his professionalism was evident. Despite his frequent informality he was an experienced master mariner and nobody was in any doubt that he was the boss.

He was relaxed with his officers, who with one exception were in their twenties or early thirties, often laughing with them, telling them stories or telling them the way of things.

He spoke to us in good, but heavily accented, English. If he had taken a little more trouble with his pronunciation his English would have been very good indeed. He did, however, suffer under the delusion that the higher the volume and the more he gesticulated the better he would be understood. He was a good talker, but a bad listener; he ignored most things you said to him. When he was in full flight that verse from the old Jimmy O'Dea monologue of the 1950s came my mind!

The Captain, a mighty man was he,
Who would stop any ship in its track,
With his father's name impressed on his mind

123

And his mother tattooed on his back.'

As his only two passengers he was considerate towards us, enquiring after a couple of days into the voyage whether as vegetarians our food was all right: 'The cook is a friend of mine and I can talk to him.' He considered himself to be a connoisseur of fish. In port when fish was needed for the ship he would go to the local market to buy it. He it was who told us that it was important to have good food on board to ensure a contented crew. One afternoon when some crew on deck not far from our cabin were chipping rust in preparation for painting, he asked us if we were going to lie down: 'I can stop the noise if you like.'

One evening Hilary and I were sitting on deck chairs outside on the wing of the bridge reading when he came out from the wheelhouse. He greeted us in a friendly way and was on for a chat. He told us that he would be leaving the ship at Salerno on the way back and as he didn't know who the new master would be we should be sure to ask him about going onto the bridge. 'Not all masters are as liberal as I am.' Hilary asked him about women at sea. He told us that there were a few junior officers and cadets: 'I'm glad I've never had any aboard, there are enough problems without that; men and women going in and out of each other's cabins.' At other times he would walk past us without even a cursory greeting.

If we were having a conversation with an officer on the bridge and the Captain was present his ears were wagging. On one occasion I was talking to the second mate who was helping me with a problem I had transferring photographs from my camera to my laptop. The Captain was out of earshot but watching. I passed him as I left the bridge when he said something to the effect that that was a serious conversation. I replied; 'We were planning a mutiny.' He came back immediately: 'You'll have to wait until Salerno to get rid of me.'

All officers must have enough English for their work; it is the international language of the sea; but of the officers only the two second mates, George from the Philippines and Raphaele from Sicily had English good enough for conversation. One of the three Filipino ABs was always on watch with an officer. They acted as helmsmen when the ship was on manual steering as we entered or left a port, and made the wonderful espresso coffee in the little pantry off the bridge. They were smiling and friendly and all three had good English. Bayani had typical Filipino jet black hair and dark skin. He spoke quietly. In a conversation with him about life at sea, we asked him what his most dramatic incident at sea had been. On a Japanese ship they had rescued six Chinese fishermen from a sinking trawler in the South China Sea. Like all seamen he was ready to talk about his family and particularly his children at home. He would prefer not to have had to go to sea but there was no work ashore.

Benjie came from a city in the Philippines, known as 'The City of Smiles.' He was a worthy citizen; his face lit up when you approached. He too had family and couldn't wait for *Gran Bretagna* to get to Antwerp where his present contract ended and from

125

where he would fly to the Philippines for three months at home with his family.

The third AB was Jesus. It is common in Spain and former Spanish colonies for boys to be christened 'Jesus'. Not only was his name Jesus, but he was Jesus Junior. He was brought up Catholic and spoke highly of the Irish nuns who ran the school to which he had gone. One of the nuns got him a job working in the convent garden with free accommodation that enabled him to go to nautical school. He had, however, become a born-again Christian. He was fascinated by the Bible and wanted to talk about it. On one occasion he engaged me in a discussion on the Bible when the Captain shouted across: 'Malana, coffee.' The Captain didn't like not knowing what we were talking about. All the Italian officers called Bayani and Benjie by their first names, but they called Jesus by his second name, Malana. To us it was strange too and we found that we didn't use his name at all. On deck one day I met Bayani looking at the metal canopy over the control console on the wing of the bridge that the three ABs had chipped and painted. I asked him if it was finished.

'No,' he said, 'Jesus has to give it a final coat.'

When they were doing the preparation work before painting, the Captain came to have a look and saw them applying mastic. He wanted to try and took the mastic gun but made a botch of it. He handed back the gun with a comment in Italian that we didn't understand and walked away.

All three ABs had spent some time at nautical school but had left before taking their exams. If their prowess at making espresso coffee was anything to go by they'd all have made excellent deck officers.

CHAPTER 2

On the second morning out of Southampton the Captain told us that in about half an hour there would be a fire drill. We went back to our cabin and took out our life-jackets, wet suits and hard hats, put on our life-jackets and waited for the alarm. When it sounded Lanzo, the steward, arrived at our cabin door also sporting his abandon-ship-regalia and we followed him to the officer and passenger lounge. We sat there for about 20 minutes until a phone call came through when Lanzo told us it was over. We went back to our cabin, put away our life-saving gear and life on board returned to normal. The following afternoon there was a crew security exercise. The Captain told us about it but said that we were not involved. We didn't see anything of it, but I had an image of crew doing a bomb search, looking for imaginary stowaways and fending off imaginary pirates.

A ship in a rough sea moves in two ways depending on the direction of the wind. As I understand it, in simple terms, if the wind is head-on to the bow, the swell causes the ship to pitch, that is to say the bow rises and falls and you may feel queasy, and if the wind is side-on, the ship rolls and you might be sick, and if the wind is somewhere between these two, the ship pitches and rolls at the same time, a corkscrew roll, and you'll be as sick as a dog. Cures for seasickness are hit and miss; what may suit one person will not suit another. I understand that 'The Ship Captain's Medical Guide,' after a dissertation on seasickness, ends: 'One might come to the conclusion that the only cure is death.' This opinion is in line with what I have heard said, that often a person with a bad bout of seasickness would be quite happy to die!

Some people are more prone to seasickness than others; from those who feel sick if they see a rough sea from dry land, to those who are not affected at all in heavy weather. I am told it is something to do with the inner ear, but it is the stomach that pays the price! There are precautions you can take, from pills that the doctor can give you to hitting yourself on the back of the head when you're not looking, and the whole gamut of other medical, old wives and nonsense cures. Seamen are not immune. They too, no matter how long they have been at sea, can be sick and between heaves they must get on with their work. Passenger liners and particularly cruise ships have stabilisers that reduce the effect of rough seas. These are for the comfort of the passengers, but they also benefit the stewards, as a fair proportion of 3,000 people getting sick all over the ship would make for a lot of extra work.

I have talked slightly humorously about seasickness, but it's really a simple matter. If you know you are seasick easily, don't go on a cargo ship voyage. On the other hand on ten weeks of cargo ship voyaging in the past two years Hilary was mildly sick once and felt queasy a few times and I felt queasy a few times too. If you begin to feel nauseous the thing to do is to go and lie down and wait until it passes.

Later on the morning of the fire drill the movement of *Gran Bretagna* increased. We were passing across the north west corner of the notorious Bay of Biscay. Hilary went and lay down and I went to lunch on my own. After lunch I lay down for a while too and in a couple of hours the wind abated and we were over it.

The following morning after breakfast we sat in deckchairs on the wing of the bridge reading in full sun under a cloudless sky. The ocean was a deep blue. A gentle breeze ruffled the surface of the water causing it to shimmer like a vast blanket of sparkling sequins to the ever present background hum of the engine as we sailed along the Portuguese coast heading for the Strait of Gibraltar and the Mediterranean Sea. Behind us on the deck glistening in the sun were row upon row of brand new cars ready for delivery to the ports on our itinerary, and in due course to traverse the roads of Southern Europe, the Middle East and North Africa.

It was roughly midnight when we approached the Strait of Gibraltar with the lights of Morocco to starboard and the lights of Spain on our port side. We could hear on the bridge radio the chatter of Moroccan fishermen passing the time as they waited for their nets to fill. The Captain piloted us between the Pillars of Hercules and set course for our first port of call, Salerno just south of the Bay of Naples.

In these days of mobile phones, keeping in touch with home is a simple matter. Ashore it is easy, but at sea there is no coverage.

On a regular route, as we were, crew members can tell you in advance the next place there will be a mobile phone signal as we pass close to an island or mainland coast. There was good coverage as we passed through the Strait, but we would not have been popular at home if we texted or phoned sometime between midnight and one in the morning! We had our next coverage as we passed close to the south coast of Sardinia on our way to Salerno. You have no difficulty knowing when you come into coverage; just keep an eye on the crew and you see some of them out on deck with mobile phones glued to their ears phoning wives, sweethearts, children, mamas or even bookies for all I know.

When we were approaching Salerno the Captain arrived onto the bridge and announced that another port had been added to our itinerary; another Turkish port in addition to Izmir, Gemlik on the Sea of Marmara not far short of Istanbul and the Bosporus. He was also exercised by information he had received from the port authorities at Salerno that we might have to lie offshore for a while; there might be a delay in allocating a berth to *Gran Bretagna*.

'Adriano, I'll phone Adriano,' he said and told us about Adriano who was a friend of his, a former master, who was now a pilot in Salerno. About an hour later we met the Captain coming out of his cabin beaming from ear to ear:

'Is there good news?' we asked.

'Yes.'

'Is it Adriano?'

'Yes, got us a berth.'

When we were in range of the harbour the pilot boat approached and the pilot boarded. When he arrived on the bridge, who was it but the bold Adriano? There was a noisy greeting between the two old friends. The Captain introduced us. Adriano spoke to us in English, he was very friendly and smiled warmly; and why wouldn't he smile, hadn't he done the business for his old friend Giovanni? It was to our advantage too, as the sooner we berthed the longer we would have ashore.

The names Bay of Naples, Sorrento, Isle of Capri, Amalfi Coast were all familiar to us, but never having been to this part of Italy we had no idea where they were in relation to each other. We were to learn. The peninsula that is the southern sweep of the Bay of Naples separates it from the bay of Salerno to the south. At the end of the peninsula separating the two bays is the Isle of Capri. Naples is on the north side of its bay and Sorrento, where the Captain was born, brought up, lives and talked of frequently, is on the south side. As we sailed into Salerno Bay we passed close to the south side of Capri, past Amalfi and along the Amalfi Coast. We could see Vesuvius in the distance and docked at the berth that Adriano had secured for us.

Ready to go ashore, we waited in the committee room for the agent and customs and security men to arrive. When the full complement of these officials arrived, at the long table sat the Captain, the third officer, three men from the ship's agents with big brief cases and wearing sweaters and jeans, and two immigration officials looking very important in navy-blue uniform with impressive braid, badges and insignia. There was another man in uniform that we judged to be important as he sat at the head of the table and seemed to conduct matters. Eventually one of the immigration men looked over to us and said in English:

'You English?'

'No,' we said, 'Irish.'

'Ah, Dublino?'

'Yes.'

'EU, no passaportos needed. Have you identification?'

'Yes,' we said, 'driving licences.' We also had our passports; we never went ashore without them EU or not.

'Good,' he said with a smile, 'have a nice day,' and we left for the lift down to the ramp to go ashore for the afternoon and evening.

I knew of Salerno as the site of the main Allied landings on the mainland of Italy after the North Africa campaign and the capture of Sicily during the Second World War. An uncle of mine had been taken prisoner of war at the Volturno River crossing north of there. It was also the site of the largest mutiny in British military history.

A contingent of approximately 300 veterans of Montgomery's Eighth Army had not gone with their units into Sicily. They were left behind in North Africa, some wounded, some with dysentery and for other reasons. When they were ready to go they were told that they were to join their former units of the Eighth Army. At sea there was a change of plan and they were to go straight to Salerno where the Americans were fighting to establish a foothold on mainland Italy. They refused to be part of the battle for Salerno and when they landed they were taken to a field where they were warned of the consequences of mutiny and over 100 of them fell into line. The remaining 191 were shipped back to North Africa where they were court-marshalled. Three NCOs were sentenced to death and the rest were sentenced to between 7 and 12 years hard labour. The sentences were soon suspended and they were sent to Salerno to join the units they had refused to join in the first place. They claimed that they had not mutinied against going into action but in order to return to their old units to fight alongside their comrades of the Eighth Army with whom they had come through the North Africa campaign.

Occasionally in port the distance from the dock to the town is such that it is easy to walk, but most often a taxi is necessary. The Captain or one of the officers will ask the agent to order a taxi in advance and in Salerno the taxi was waiting at the ramp and dropped us at an internet point in the middle of the town. On most cargo vessels passengers and crew do not have direct access to e-mail or the internet. The Captain, however, does and usually with permission passengers may use it, but it is such a palaver it is not worth the trouble unless absolutely necessary. Some Scandinavian lines have recently begun to make internet available to all crew and passengers on board.

There was a settlement at Salerno from ancient times. What is reputed to have been the earliest medical school in Europe was started there in the 11th century. You can see a permanent exhibition of its activity between the 11th and 13th centuries. Much of the *centro storico*, the historic centre, survived serious damage during the war. We rambled around the centre absorbing the atmosphere of the place, and Hilary occasionally looked in the window of a clothes or shoe shop to compare prices with home.

At sea there is no choice at meals; you take what you get, and in our case, even as vegetarians, what we got was good. However one of the things we looked forward to when we went ashore was to go to a restaurant for something different from ship's fare. In the centre of Salerno when we went to look for a restaurant we couldn't find one; plenty of cafes, pizzerias and coffee bars but not a proper restaurant anywhere. Eventually we found one up a side street. It was approximately 6.30 pm and as we approached we were unsure if it was open until we tried the door. To our great relief it was. There was nobody else there.

Here I must digress and, for the benefit of carnivores, recount the vicissitudes of vegetarians eating out. Vegetarians, gastronomically, are second class citizens. Normally when going to a restaurant we would phone ahead and say we are vegetarians and the response is usually something to the effect:

'That is no problem, sir. We cater for vegetarians.'

When the waiter arrives and you say you are vegetarian he proudly points to the only vegetarian item on the menu which is more than likely to be risotto or kedgeree or one of an infinite variety of pastas. When you say: 'But there is no choice, the carnivores have six options,' the waiter is quite likely to say: 'What would you like, sir? We can do you a cheese or mushroom omelette.' For chefs, rice, pasta and omelette are the three cop-out vegetarian dishes. You bite your tongue and say inside your head: 'Would you ever go to hell? I'll never come to this bloody restaurant again.' If it is just the two of you, you could get up and walk out, and if you do get a table somewhere else, when you arrive it is likely to be the same story, and you're hungry and won't get food for at least another hour. If you are with friends, you don't want to make a fuss and for one reason or another you take the dish on offer.

When vegetarians go to a party and it comes to the buffet supper your hostess points to a dish on the table and says proudly: 'This is vegetarian.' You thank her, take some and go and sit down somewhere. It's very tasty so you go back for a little more, but it's all gone. The bloody carnivores have scoffed the lot. Again you swear inside your head. The moral of the story is: if you are a vegetarian the only satisfactory place to eat is at home!

Now to return to the only restaurant we could find in Salerno. We went in and the middle-aged waitress approached. We drew on our minute store of practical Italian just to be sure there was no misunderstanding and said: '*Siamo vegetariani. Ne carne, ne pesce.*' A phrase we learned by rote the first time we went to Italy: 'We are vegetarians. No meat, no fish.' She had no English and pulling out two chairs at a table gestured that there was no problem. We knew that there was no chance of getting vegetarian food, but we could have something that wasn't meat or fish. To keep life simple, since in Italian the word for omelette is *omelette* we asked if we could have cheese omelettes. She smiled and nodded enthusiastically. Having had so much pasta on board we craved a spud and ordered roast potatoes. In Italy they do wonderful diced potato roasted in duck fat. Though vegetarians we are not bigots! In due course the waitress arrived with what transpired to be lasagne, lasagne without meat, be it said, and straight from the freezer, with three or four small pieces of barely roasted potato each. *Delizioso*, she said as she put it before us. She also told us it was the best restaurant in Salerno. We took the line of least resistance, said nothing, not that she would have understood if we had, and ate the lasagne, which was OK, but it wasn't omelette in any language.

For dessert, being in Italy, we took the opportunity to have ice cream. The Italians make some of the best ice cream you can have anywhere. Again we called on our meagre knowledge of Italian and ordered *gelato*. The waitress smiled again and nodded. She arrived back with what we discovered later is called *semifreddo*; layers of sponge cake with fruit and a thin layer of ice cream in the middle. We paid the bill and left, glad to return to the ship where Lanzo the cook, provided good basic but tasty vegetarian meals. On the way back in the taxi the mystery of the dearth of restaurants was solved. There were restaurants galore just outside the town on the road back to the dock. When we arrived back there was a meal in progress in the mess for some officers, wives and girlfriends; Salerno is the home port of the Grimaldi Line and we weren't sailing until morning.

In the morning we went to the top deck and watched the quay below as some of the cargo of cars, not much bigger than Dinkies from that height, were driven down the ramp, along the quay and parked in neat rows ready for the big road car transporters to load them in due course and distribute them to dealers in the region. The discharging complete, the pilot on board (not Adriano this time), we cast off and moved slowly away from the quay, out into the harbour and into the bay. The pilot ready to leave the bridge, the deck cadet, Agostino, gave him from one of the chart drawers a carton of cigarettes, the traditional gift from this ship to a departing pilot. Smoking at sea is an occupational hazard! One of the officers counted for me when I asked: 23 out of a crew of 26 on *Gran Bretagna* were smokers.

We set course south towards the Strait of Messina between Italy and Sicily, Scylla and Charybdis of Greek mythology. Scylla was a monster on a rock with six heads on the end of long necks. Charybdis was a monster that sucked in vast quantities of water and spewed it out creating a treacherous whirlpool. The mariner had to choose to which he would go closer while passing through the Strait. Homer had Odysseus choose Scylla on the grounds that he might lose only a few sailors rather than risk Charybdis and lose his whole ship. He navigates the Strait successfully but loses six of his best sailors to the tentacles of Scylla. In *Ulysses* Joyce places his Scylla and Charybdis episode in the National Library, where Stephen propounds his Hamlet theory. During it he uses the options of choosing from two extremes exemplified by the logical grounded Aristotle symbolised by Scylla's rock and the abstract forms or ideas of Plato symbolised by Charybdis, the whirlpool.

There was storm force 9 wind and we were in for the second and last passage of heavy seas of our voyage. Moving around the cabin was hazardous – one minute being flung one way and in a split second holding on to something to avoid being flung the other. We both felt queasy and lay down on our bed. After a while we felt we ought to put something into our stomachs and ventured down to the mess holding on carefully to the hand-rail along the alleyway. In the mess the Captain was presiding at the long table. He invited us to join him, the chief engineer and four or five officers tucking in to large portions of pizza. We took a little in the hope of settling our stomachs and quickly retreated to our cabin and got into bed. The ship was still pitching and rolling, the cabin creaked and every now and then a large wave hit the ship and caused all 51,000 tons of her to shudder like a lightly built out-half that was checked by a 20 stone front row forward. One loud thud and shudder felt as if some huge solid thing had hit the hull of the ship, but it could only have been a wave. The wind would ease and then build up again and drive cascades of rain against the cabin window. We eventually fell asleep. The Captain recounted to us in the morning that the sea was so rough the pilot to bring us through the Strait of Messina couldn't board, as was practice, three miles north of the Strait and had to wait to board until we had entered the actual Strait. Having passed through we turned left (to port!)

east across the Ionian Sea and passed along the south coast of Greece and then north to Piraeus, the port of Athens.

We talk of the calm before the storm. On the bridge in the morning while we relished the calm after the storm, there was a telegraph from the Italian coastguard asking shipping to keep a lookout for a lone yachtsman in a yellow hulled yacht in the Ionian Sea. He had set out from Ithica to sail to Crotone, a port on the boot of Italy, and later he had sent out a distress signal and then nothing further. We would never know if this sailor had been rescued or lost.

When we arrived in the mess for breakfast, Lanzo the cook put his head around the door from the galley:

'A good day today,' Hilary said, 'better than last night.'

He replied: 'Last night, very problem.'

After breakfast, on the wing of the bridge, I looked down the deck and saw Gussie, the young deck cadet, leaning on the rail looking out to sea in contemplative mode. He was not much more than 20 years old and sometimes he gave the impression of being a bit at sea, if you'll excuse the pun. What was he thinking? I'll never stick this, I love this life, or was he thinking of a girl or maybe his mama. As I watched he looked up and waved. I waved back and I wondered.

Chapter 3

We docked in Piraeus at about 7.30 am. It is the largest passenger port in Europe and is almost a suburb of Athens; 9 miles from the centre. The agent was on board quickly and we were ashore by about 8.30 am. Foolishly we hadn't asked the agent to order a taxi, so we made our own way towards the dock exit and were lost. We finally found our way to a main road, hailed a taxi and went the half hour journey to the centre of Athens. The taxi driver dropped us at Syntagma Square which is overlooked by the Parliament Building. We watched the soldiers in front of the parliament in traditional dress, pleated skirts, shoes with pompoms and rifles on their shoulders, strutting their stuff.

This square is the centre of demonstrations against the measures that the Greek government took in an effort to ensure that their national economy did not collapse completely in the recession. In these demonstrations people have been killed. In Dublin there have been no similar demonstrations against the harsh measures the government has taken because of the reckless behaviour of bankers, developers and their political cronies that wrecked the economy in pursuit of their own greed and to fill their own pathetic ego needs.

These geniuses landed us all in the worst economic crisis ever and forced ordinary decent hard working taxpayers to bail them out. They are supposed to be the elite of our society and I am sure there were many sound economic principles they chose to ignore but the simplest of all that they ignored was: what goes up must come down. Every child over the age of about six knows that. However when this was pointed out to Bertie Ahern, the Taoiseach, he said that people who said this kind of thing should commit suicide. The fact of the matter is that if anybody should commit suicide it should have been he for destroying the economy and causing hardship and misery to a large proportion of the population.

In a restaurant just off the square having coffee we wondered how far we were from the Acropolis. Without even having discussed it we both assumed that we wouldn't have time to go there. We asked the waitress how far it was. 'One stop on the metro.' We finished our coffee quickly, paid the bill and went back to Syntagma Square, down to the metro and in 20 minutes we were on the Acropolis, (ancient Greek for high point of the city), and half way up the hill to the Parthenon (*parthenos*: virgin) a temple dedicated to Athena, the virgin goddess and patron of Athens after whom the city is named. Originally the Parthenon housed a huge gold and ivory statue of Athena. The Parthenon was completed in 432 BC, at the high point of Greek civilisation, and contains all the finest features of Greek architecture. When we saw it, it was surrounded by scaffolding and some giant cranes; part of the programme of maintenance of this unique ancient monument. It was also surrounded by hundreds of tourists from two cruise ships docked at the passenger terminal in Piraeus. Keeping an eye on our time we made our way down to the Acropolis metro station and back to the city centre to get a taxi to Piraeus.

Here I digress to ride a hobby horse of mine. I am suspicious of all taxi drivers. Taxi drivers have ripped me off, tried to rip me off and no doubt in many instances I have not been aware of, have succeeded in ripping me off, in many cities in different parts of the world. Years ago in the days of our innocence, in New York Hilary and I hailed a cab and asked for the docks where we were to board a liner to Cobh. When we arrived at the dock the driver asked for some phenomenal fare for the journey. We looked for the meter. It was turned off and he gave us some guff about it being cheaper to quote a fare, which he hadn't done. We gave him half what he asked and he drove off cursing and swearing at us. A favourite ploy when a driver knows you are a stranger is to drive you on a circuitous route to get a bigger fare.

In Rome on one occasion we had walked a good distance from our hotel, found we were too tired to walk back so we hailed a taxi. It was soon clear that he was driving us all around the world not for sport, but for a bigger fare. When he stopped at our hotel and quoted the fare on the meter, I let him know that I knew what he had done. I took out a piece of paper and a biro and told him I wanted to take his number. I stood back on the footpath to look for his number on the roof and he took off without any fare!

A friend arriving in a strange city took a taxi from the station to her hotel. It took about twenty minutes. A few days later when she was checking out she asked the receptionist to order a taxi to the station to be told that she wouldn't need a taxi; the station was just around the corner.

I once got out of a taxi on Tara Street in Dublin. I stood out and handed a note to the driver through the front passenger window. The driver put his boot down and disappeared like a shot around the corner onto the quay leaving me gobsmacked and without my change. Despite all of this, I readily acknowledge that there must be a few fine upstanding honourable taxi drivers somewhere in the world. The rest are shysters.

When you stand at a taxi rank and wait your turn, you can be lucky or unlucky in the taxi driver you get. That day in the centre of Athens going back to our ship we were unlucky. The driver we got didn't try to diddle us out of money, but he was not pleasant nor was he bright. We sat into the back and asked for Piraeus, Ikonio Dock. We were always careful to note the name of the dock when leaving the ship. He didn't reply, but gestured to indicate that he understood. We then told him explicitly that it was not a passenger dock but a commercial one. There was a notice in English in the front of the car: 'PLEASE USE YOUR SAFETY BELT.' We could not find safety belts in the back. We asked in case we were missing them. 'None,' he replied. After a few minutes he lit a cigarette, which we ignored. In another ten minutes he lit another. Hilary asked him if he would mind not smoking. 'Sorry,' he said and put the cigarette out. The next part of the journey as we came into Piraeus was uneventful, until we came to a large overhead sign that said: 'PASSENGER TERMINAL.' In measured tones I told him again that we didn't want the passenger terminal, but a commercial dock named Ikonio. He pulled over and asked another taxi driver for directions and turned the car. At the next traffic lights he asked a truck driver beside him for more directions, and on we went. He stopped and asked two more people the way and he was still lost when we saw *Gran Bretagna* in the distance. We paid him the figure on the meter and we were relieved to be 'home.'

Still in port, we went to the mess for dinner at the usual time of 6.00 pm. The chief engineer had been at it again! Vincenzo, the chief engineer was a small, round, bald man who smiled a warm smile when he met us, and sang to himself as he went about the ship. He hadn't a word of English. Maybe he knew the English words for the parts of a marine engine and for how it worked, but needless to say an occasion for us to discuss these things with him didn't arise. In fact we knew nothing about the engine except the sound and the smell. The sound was always there in the background, and that lovely smell of a warm engine wafted out from the vents and from the entrance to the engine room, which was always open, on our deck two thirds of the way towards the stern. We passed them when we went for a walk for some exercise or to stand at the stern and watch the mesmeric patterns of the wash. The wash, the disturbance of the sea made by the action of the propeller, stretched in a long line behind the ship, the pattern diminishing and finally disappearing into the surface of the sea leaving no trace of our course.

A pastime of the chief engineer while at sea was to make the most delightful and professional standard pastries, éclairs, bonne bouche and cream filled cornets. These appeared from time to time for dessert. Lanzo, steward, sported a big smile when he arrived at table with the engineer's pastries. He knew that we got a bit bored with fresh fruit for dessert. Leaving the mess one evening that we had had the pastries I put my head around the door of the galley and asked Lanzo, the cook, if he ever helped the chief engineer in the engine room. His vacant response told me that either he didn't understand what I said or didn't think it was funny!

Later that night when we were at sea, bound for Izmir, Turkey, the Captain informed us that our call to Gemlik, near the Bosporus, which had been added to our itinerary a few days earlier, had been cancelled. He also asked us in a kindly way if, when we approached Izmir, we would mind leaving the bridge as the pilots in Izmir are very nervous and excitable.

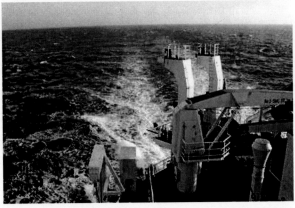

CHAPTER 4

We moored in the harbour at Izmir for about three hours before going to the quay. After our difficulty finding our way out of the dock at Piraeus, you would think we would have had the sense to order a taxi, but the ship's agent gave us directions to the passenger exit and he assured us that it was easy to find. We left the ship and spent at least half an hour looking for the pedestrian exit in a dock that seemed to us to be much more extensive than the dock at Piraeus. We finally found it and took a taxi to the centre of town. The one thing I had to do was find a camera shop as my camera had packed up in Athens. As we stepped out of the taxi a friendly middle-aged man, well dressed, approached us, asked us where we were from, made polite conversation and welcomed us to Izmir. We asked him if he would direct us to a camera shop. He called over a young man from the shop door behind him and said: 'This is my nephew, he will help you.' The young man also was friendly and brought us to a camera shop a couple of streets away. We thanked him, but he said that he would wait in case there was anything else we wanted. When we had bought a new camera he wanted to bring us to his uncle's shop selling high quality and designer clothes. We thanked him again for his help and said firmly that we would not need him any further. Reluctantly he left us and we wandered on along the street enjoying the feel of the place.

Suddenly Hilary fell across in front of me and hit the footpath on her face. She had tripped over the kerb of a flower bed. Blood poured from her nose and on the outside it was cut. We got her onto her knees, squeezed her nose with a handkerchief and before we knew, a stool appeared from somewhere that she sat on with her back to a lamppost. Three or four more men arrived; two gave us bottles of water, two or three packets of moist wipes appeared, one man went away and came back with a plastic bag full of ice, which we used to stem the bleeding. Hilary was shaken, and so was I. She sat on the stool gathering herself together. A couple of the men kept saying 'hospital' 'no charge.' I assume they thought we were declining to go because of cost. Hilary protested that she would be all right. A man arrived with a wad of tissues and sprinkled them liberally from a bottle of Eau de Cologne. This gave Hilary great relief. Though quite badly cut on her nose the bleeding had stopped and she was beginning to feel a little bit better when we heard an ambulance at the end of the street. The street was too narrow for the ambulance to enter. Two young paramedics arrived and one took Hilary's blood pressure. It was fine, but she finally conceded that she would go to the hospital.

She got into the back of the ambulance with the two paramedics, while I climbed into the cab with the driver. We took off, siren blaring, through chaotic traffic. Hilary lay on a trolley but they did not strap her on, so when we started to move she was shaken from side to side. Up in the cab I watched as traffic pulled in to let us pass and we went through a couple of red lights. In six or seven minutes we were at the hospital. A wheelchair arrived and they took Hilary in to A & E, where she was seen immediately. A porter brought me to a hatch where I gave her details and paid €15, and then he brought me to where Hilary was surrounded by a middle-aged woman doctor with dyed blonde hair and heavily made up, a male paramedic and two young nurses, all trying to ask questions with very limited English, the sum total of which was to discover if she fell because she had a weakness or because she tripped. The doctor gave her an anti-tetanus injection and wanted her to have an X-ray of her nose, but Hilary declined as she reckoned that it wasn't broken and even if it had been, there was nothing they could do. She signed a form to say she had declined an X-ray and we left with smiles and handshakes all round. We found a comfortable restaurant nearby that the doctor had recommended, sat outside with cups of coffee and watched the world of down-town Izmir go by.

With plenty of time in hand we took a taxi and when we got out at the passenger gate of the dock a man in uniform rushed towards us:

'Come, quick. In time.' A large cruise ship we could see from the gate was preparing to sail. We explained that we were on a cargo vessel and when he saw the plaster on Hilary's nose and her two black eyes he was very solicitous:

'Sit there, I get car to bring you to ship.' He called up a man in a little car who in a couple of minutes drove us through the dock in which we had earlier been lost, to *Gran Bretagna*, and once more we were glad to be 'home.' Later on when the Captain saw the walking wounded his main concern was that the accident hadn't happened on board. We were due to sail at 7.00pm, but we were still loading when we went to bed at 10.30 pm.

We sailed at midnight. In the morning we passed islands with Greek sounding names, some of them familiar, that are closer to the Turkish coast than to the Greek mainland: Chios, Samos, Ikaria, Leros, Kos off the coast of Bodrum, a popular Turkish resort where, in the so-called good times, Irish people bought apartments, and Rhodes famous for its Colossus, one of the Seven Wonders of the Ancient World. We sat on our deckchairs in the warm Aegean sun, cloudless sky, deep blue sea, on the deck of our moving island, *Gran Bretagna*, on our way to the Mediterranean and Cyprus.

CHAPTER 5

The first time Cyprus ever came to my notice was when I was a small boy in one of the early years of the 1950s. I took 'The Irish Times' from our letterbox, opened it and there on the front page was the photograph of a scene where a British soldier in mufti had been shot in the back by a terrorist as he walked with his wife on a city street in Cyprus. I don't remember which city. Beside it was a report and a photograph of Archbishop Makarios, the leader of the Cypriot political movement for independence from Britain. I remember wondering at an archbishop being so involved in politics, what I now know to be the insidious involvement of Church with State. I remember liking the sound of his name, which I later learned meant Archbishop Blesséd.

Little did I think as a boy, after World War II, when it was a wonder of wonders that the son of friends of my parents was going on a holiday to Majorca, rather than to the Wexford seaside towns of Rosslare or Courtown, that one day I would travel to all the places around the world, on four continents, that air travel and now travel by sea would enable me to reach. Here I was heading for the homeland of that impressive, bearded and robed churchman/politician Archbishop Blesséd. Of course much has happened since Cyprus gained its independence from Britain in 1960. Like Ireland the population consisted of two ethnic communities, in this case Greek and Turkish, and in 1974 after years of violence Turkey invaded the island and it is now partitioned with the Turks in the north and the Greeks in the south. There is a buffer zone between the two and ne'er the twain shall meet. They are even further apart today, physically, politically and socially than the north and south of Ireland were even in the 1950s.

We took a taxi to down town Limassol and wandered around. We found an internet point to keep in touch with the big bad world, and found in a shop real sponges. Both of us remembered them from when we were children, but neither of us had seen one for many years. For younger people who may not know, they are the original sponge from the bottom of the sea and are soft and gentle to use. We bought one for our new granddaughter, for her bath. Subsequently somebody told us that trade in natural sponges is illegal. We hope she won't be arrested! We found a supermarket and bought teabags, cereal as a break from the cornflakes supplied on board and some Mars bars to indulge my periodic craving for something sweet and to help me to work, rest and play.

Limassol was not the most inspiring of towns, and furthermore around almost every corner there were barriers to stop pedestrians falling into holes made for some kind of abandoned road, water or sewage works. The exception was the promenade. It was long and beautifully kept: palm trees, shrubs clipped and grass cut. We found a good restaurant there and had an excellent lunch looking across the harbour. We saw no sign of Archbishop Makarios. There is, I understand, a fine statue of him somewhere but we didn't see it.

When the time came to return to the ship we hailed a taxi. The driver was chatty and despite telling him that we were on a cargo vessel and where to find it and despite telling him, when he asked, that there were only two passengers on board, where do you think he drove us? To the passenger entrance to a big cruise liner that was in port. This was the third time that, despite our appearance and instructions, we had been mistaken for well heeled, cosseted and highly organised voyagers on luxury floating hotels.

Later in the day we sailed for Alexandria, Egypt, which was named after Alexander the Great who founded the city on the Nile delta. It was the capital of ancient Egypt and in its harbour there had been another of the Seven Wonders of the Ancient World - the Pharos Lighthouse. It was built in the 3rd century BC and was the tallest building in the then world. During the 4th and 14th centuries it had been damaged by earthquakes. It finally collapsed into ruin in 1346. Alexandria also contained the largest library in the ancient world, which was destroyed by fire. A modern library built on the ancient site was opened in 2002. Today the city is the first port and second city of Egypt.

Even before we arrived at Limassol there was mention on the bridge of Alexandria. We were told that it was not like any of our other ports of call; passengers were not allowed to go ashore there. It was clear to us, though it wasn't put in so many words that there was too much bureaucracy. Passengers going ashore would have to negotiate a labyrinth of Arab officialdom and all that goes with it that would leave them with precious little or even no time to see or do anything.

The usual carton of cigarettes for the pilot on leaving the bridge had a new dimension in Egypt. The deck cadet and one of the officers prepared three black sacks each containing seven or eight cartons, one sack for the pilot and two for officials ashore. The officer explained to us that if these men were not encouraged in this way they would find some minor mistake or irregularity in documentation that would delay the ship. So much so were cigarettes a present that helped to avoid delays that the officers referred to Alexandria as 'Marlborough Country.'

When we arrived we were delayed 14 hours at anchor in the bay waiting for a pilot to board. There was no Adriano in Alexandria! At discreet intervals the officer on watch would call the pilot station on some pretext to remind them that *Gran Bretagna* was still waiting. At one stage during this time from the deck below I could hear the Captain shouting on the bridge. I had no doubt that he was ranting against the way Alexandrian port officials had of conducting business.

Eventually late at night we berthed at the quay, and by the time we were up for breakfast in the morning we were ready to sail. We stood on the deck and watched as tugs manoeuvred us slowly away from the wharf. Bayani pointed out to us a large significant looking building as one of President Mubarak's palaces. I had been in

Alexandria seven or eight years previously, arriving by road from Cairo, and I was sorry that Hilary had not had the opportunity to see it.

We sailed north-eastward; our destination Ashdod, Israel. At sea it was hot, probably in the late 30s centigrade. By evening it had cooled slightly but it was still hot. We sat in the shade on deck and surveyed the vast expanse of smooth blue sea and not another ship in sight. We were no more than a speck of a speck on planet earth, which itself is but a speck of a speck in one solar system in one of billions of galaxies in this wonderful and mysterious universe.

As we sat there the Captain emerged from the wheelhouse. While we listened to him it became clear that there was something in particular that he wanted to broach. He told us again that he would be leaving the ship at Salerno on the way back. There would be a new Captain and he reminded us to be sure to ask him for permission to go onto the bridge. He did not know who the new Captain would be, but reiterated that not all Captains were as liberal as he was in giving this permission to passengers. We had the feeling that there was a particular Captain in the line that would not allow passengers on the bridge and he was preparing us in case it might be he that took over in Salerno. We appreciated his advice and said that of course we would be careful to ask the new master as we had asked him when we had boarded in the first place when his response had been: 'Yes, you can go on the bridge.'

Later we checked the brochure we had received from the company when we had booked the passage, which under

'BRIDGE' said: 'Under the ISPS (International Ship and Port Security) code the bridge is a restricted area, where, in general, access cannot be allowed. We appreciate that our passengers enjoy being on the bridge, but please ask the master for authorisation for any visit to the bridge. Please respect the dress code.' Under 'DRESS CODE' it said: 'No bathing suit or beachwear should be worn in the mess room and lounge. Do not enter the bridge in beachwear or bathing suit.' As is often the case, things are more relaxed in practice then they are in the regulations and to ask the Captain for permission for every visit is simply impractical, but it is not unreasonable that the dress code should be observed to the letter.

We knew from the second officer, Georgio, that while in port in Ashdod we would have plenty of time to get to Jerusalem which was one hour away. This we planned to do. Before we went to bed, the third officer explained to us that we were due to dock at approximately 3.00 am. An Israeli security official would arrive to put all personnel on board through a security check. We would be called at about 3.30 am. We were fast asleep when at 3.30 am precisely we were wakened by a telephone call from the Captain asking us to go to the meeting room. Half asleep, we pulled clothes over our nightwear and when we arrived we found crew of all ranks standing in the alleyway outside the meeting room like schoolboys waiting to be interviewed outside the headmaster's study. We joined the queue making polite conversation; the kind you do when you're wakened at 3.30 am! In due course our names were called. We went in to find the Captain in full uniform sitting at the head of the long table and to his right sat a beautiful young woman in her mid twenties, head and shoulders visible over a large machine on the table in front of her. The Captain introduced us. The security officer smiled and in a kindly and gentle voice asked if we had brought our passports. The Captain had them and gave them to her. She inspected them, recorded them and handed them back. Then she asked us to record our thumbprints on a little gadget on the table and to look at the camera mounted to the side of the machine to have our mugshots taken. This delightful young woman was disarming as she asked us some questions, which was no doubt the idea.

'Do you intend to go ashore?'

'Yes. We are hoping to get to Jerusalem.'

'What do you want to see?' The only thing I could think of was the Wailing Wall, but I remembered that that was considered by some to be a pejorative name and the politically correct term nowadays was Western Wall.

'The Western Wall,' I replied.

'The usual tourist attractions,' she added. 'Do you know anybody who lives in Israel?' We both thought and said:

'No, not that we can think of.'

'Will you be carrying anything that might be mistaken for a gun?' We both smiled and said:

'No.' Then I remembered my walking stick with a seat, that breaks into three and fits into its little green bag on my back. I use it to rest my mildly arthritic lower back on tourist trips. She smiled and said:

'That will be all right. Your shore passes will be at the ramp in the morning and don't forget your passports.' We thanked her, relieved that she didn't consider either of us a security risk.

We went back to bed and had about an hour's sleep before our alarm clock woke us in time to be down at the ramp at 6.45 am for the taxi that the agent had ordered to take us to Jerusalem.

We picked up our shore passes from the AB on duty at the ramp and the taxi was already there. When our driver-cum-guide saw us approaching he stood out of the cab and shook hands with us:

'My name is Eyal.'

'Pat and Hilary.'

Eyal was in his early forties, average height, oval face, short dark hair, navy tee shirt, jeans and a diffident smile. We set off. The official at the port exit scrutinised our passes, went into the office, came out again and waved us through. Eyal asked us where we were from. We told him, Ireland, and in case that might have particular religious associations in his mind I added that we weren't particularly religious so he didn't need to put that slant on our visit to Jerusalem. But then what else is there for a visitor to Jerusalem, but the religious? He told us that he was a non-religious, secular Jew. He had lived abroad for a fair part of his life: Canada, New Zealand, Australia and the Philippines, and he had served a spell in the Israeli Army.

As we left Ashdod on a motorway, the impression of the countryside was of an all over sunburnt brown, interspersed with well cultivated, irrigated fields of vegetables and sunflower. The most striking thing was that there were only small discreet names to identify businesses and hotels. There were no advertising hoardings or large advertisements of any kind.

Eyal had very good English and our conversation was relaxed and open. In particular we asked him about state health, education and welfare services. We asked him about Jew/Arab relations within Israel. He told us that Israeli Arabs were in the main good citizens. In a little while he pointed to a village off the motorway.

'That's an Arab village. Never any trouble.'

I wanted to get a photograph, a fixing shot of a road sign saying 'Jerusalem.' Eyal slowed down, but being on a motorway he couldn't stop. With my new camera I was slow.

'Just zoom 'n shoot,' he said. Being uncertain of his name at first, we called him Zoom 'n Shoot and later on he used it of himself a couple of times. He was good fun and as a guide he was a pleasure to be with.

At this stage I need to come clean about my attitude to what are known as the Holy Sites. When I was ordained and active in the ministry of the Church, I had no interest whatever in seeing the putative sites of the life of Jesus. Visiting them would not have strengthened, reinforced or influenced in any way what I believed. The concept of pilgrimage meant nothing to me. Not only that, but having read about them and having heard them discussed, I was completely sceptical about their authenticity. I felt about them the same way that I felt about relics; items like pieces of the true cross, so called surviving pieces of the foreskin of Jesus, bones of saints, the Turin Shroud and a million other things to which devout people give great reverence and claim that they have value as catalysts to getting closer to God or even miracles. To me they were all likely to be ordinary items that became objects of pure superstition. I believed that none of these things is what it is claimed to be. In my opinion they were fake. It defies reason and commonsense that the originals of most if not all of these things could have survived, and even if some of them are genuine, it is a strange kind of God that would be influenced by faith in or devotion to them by those who have access to them over the faith and devotion of people who don't.

Our first stop in Jerusalem was at the Garden of Gethsemane. Eyal parked and directed us up the hill to the entrance. The garden at the foot of the Mount of Olives is now enclosed by walls. The New Testament account says that it is the place where on the night of his arrest Jesus went with his disciples to pray. He went a little way apart on his own and his sweat was like drops of blood as he prayed that this cup would pass from him. While he was alone the disciples fell asleep. He wakened them and they fell asleep again. Then Judas arrived with the soldiers and betrayed Jesus with a kiss. Peter cut off the ear of a servant of the High Priest and Jesus healed it miraculously. He was then taken away for trial.

Today it is a lovely small, walled garden containing ancient gnarled olive trees, from where you can look across the valley to the city of Jerusalem behind a part of the ancient wall. As we walked around the garden I saw a gardener with his back to us relieving himself against one of the trees. When he finished he came in our direction and I asked him how old the trees were. 'Two thousand years old,' he replied. What a coincidence, how convenient! Literature I consulted on the matter since we came home says that some of them may be as much as 900 years old. Other sources say that some of them were saplings when Jesus was there. People are inclined to say anything, true or false, that will bolster the case they want to make. Apparently the arborists cannot help because olive trees are not amenable to dating like other trees. In California years ago I was told that the giant redwoods are the only living things in the world today that were alive in the time of Jesus.

Beside the garden there is a Franciscan monastery and a Roman Catholic church, The Church of All Nations, which is built on the spot where Jesus is said to have been arrested. The spot is visible, marked and roped off in the basement. How in the name of all that's wonderful could anybody know this? Somebody along the way said it without a shred of evidence, somebody else believed them and in no time it became tradition and for the pious it took on devotional significance or even became, like many of the other putative sites, a catalyst for miracle or spiritual benefit. Across the valley in the old city of Jerusalem on the Temple Mount is the spot from which Muslims believe that Mohammad ascended into heaven.

We returned to the car and Eyal directed us down steep steps to the tomb of Mary, where a priest, Roman Catholic, Orthodox or Armenian we didn't know, was about to say Mass. There were people praying, kissing stones, pictures and altars. There were petitions written on pieces of paper shoved into corners and cracks around the tomb. We had seen this practice in a museum in China where petitions on scraps of paper had been shoved into glass cases containing ancient Buddhas through gaps where the wooden frame had come away from the glass. Similar petitions are left at holy wells in remote parts of rural Ireland. There seems to be a universal belief that dead holy people can somehow help ordinary living people with the problems of life. I wondered how Roman Catholicism viewed the tomb of Mary when that Church has a doctrine which says Mary, mother of Jesus, having died was assumed body and soul into heaven. However this belief seems not to have been known in the first three centuries of the Church. Furthermore it is difficult to understand how a physical body could be assumed into a spiritual realm.

After the tomb of Mary we crossed the Kedron Valley and entered the old city of Jerusalem. We hadn't had time to have breakfast before we left the ship, so the first item on our agenda was to find a café or restaurant.

'I know the very place,' Eyal said and brought us to a small café that sold bagels exclusively. There were different kinds of bagel and six or eight different fillings. As the woman behind the counter told us what the different fillings were, we couldn't believe our ears. She pointed to one and said: 'scallion and cream cheese.' When Tesco first came to Ireland they sold what they called 'spring onions,' the English name for scallions, and here we were in Jerusalem where there was scallion in cream cheese as a filler for bagels in a café that must have had some Irish connection. We explained this to Eyal who was fascinated. The bagels were excellent and we wandered down through the Armenian Quarter towards the Wailing Wall.

We could see the top of the Wall as we went down the hill and had a fine view to the Temple Mount and the Dome of the Rock behind it. The Temple Mount is the third most holy place in the world for Muslims after Mecca and Medina. At the end of the Six Days War in 1967 when the Israelis had captured Jordanian governed Jerusalem, the soldiers ran the Israeli flag up on the Mount. Immediately General Moshe Dayan ordered them to take it down in the interest of ethnic and community relations. Today the Mount is controlled by the Muslims, but has significance for Jews as the putative location of the Holy of Holies of the second Temple which was destroyed by the Romans in 70 AD. The name 'Weeping Wall' came from the weeping and wailing for the destruction of the Temple and the diaspora of the Jews. It is also a holy place, but of lesser significance, to Christians as a place associated with the life of Jesus.

While the Jordanians controlled this part of Jerusalem, Jews did not have access to the Temple Mount which they believe held the

Holy of Holies of the second Temple. The closest they could get was to this wall below the Mount that they believed to be the last surviving wall of the second Temple and so it became for them a holy place. They were even forbidden access to the Wall between 1948 and 1967.

As Eyal and I approached the Wall we were given disposable skull caps to wear. Hilary had to go to the Wall itself through the women's section which gave access to about a third of its length. It was marked off from the men's two thirds by a six foot fence at right angles to the Wall. Eyal and I stood back and watched the men, many in the black suits, hats and the ringlets of Orthodox Jews, some who wore prayer shawls, others in jeans and ordinary day wear, as they stood up to the Wall praying, reading from holy books, many of them rocking as though in a trance. There were two soldiers in uniform, automatic weapons slung over their shoulders, kit bags beside them on the ground, leaning against the Wall praying. There were petitions on paper in cracks between the stones. There is a free e-mail service available to Jews from around the world to have their petitions placed in the cracks. All the petitions are removed and disposed of at the end of each day. There were small tables and plastic patio type chairs back from the Wall where groups sat and there were small groups of men standing talking and others just wandering around. There were a number of prie-dieus that nobody seemed to use. Eyal insisted that I should stand beside the wall, I hasten to add facing back towards him, while he took a photograph.

Near us a teacher was giving instruction from a holy book to a group of twelve or fourteen five or six year old children sitting in a circle on the ground. This is the practice of most religions; to indoctrinate their children as early as possible. They inculcate their innocent and vulnerable minds with the religious concepts and beliefs of their 'tribe,' on the principle of the Jesuits: 'Give me a child till he's seven and he'll be a Catholic for life.' Modern psychology supports the view that the principle behind this is so, that what is absorbed in the early years is formative and perhaps even indelible. Some people say that this early religious indoctrination of children is a form of child abuse. Hilary returned and described the ecstatic state of some of the women at the section of the wall where she was. The whole atmosphere of the place was unreal. Depending on your point of view, it could be seen as a highly significant tribal shrine or as an open air lunatic asylum.

We left the Wall and went through the streets of the old city with their wonderful atmosphere, all beautifully paved in stone, until we came to the Via Dolorosa, the Way of Sorrows. This is said to be the way that Jesus went to the place of his crucifixion. According to Matthew, Mark and Luke, Simon of Cyrene carried his cross, according to John Jesus carried his own cross. This, and Golgotha to where it led, could not have been more different from my childhood and lifetime mental picture of them. I knew of course that today they were part of the city and not the dusty desert regions of 2,000 years ago, but when I was actually there I was even more incredulous of the Holy Sites than I had been before. On the Via Dolorosa there is a stone set into the wall in which there is what could be construed as a handprint that the pious believe to be the handprint of Jesus.

We went up the street with its shops and stalls doing normal business; traders standing at their doors trying to encourage people to buy. They all used some version of: 'Come and look, if you don't buy we will still like you, but if you do buy we will like you even more.' From one of the stalls Eyal bought and shared with us a bag of freshly made falafels, just as at home you would buy a bag of chips. They were delicious. Along the street are marked the Stations of the Cross. This is where on Christian feast days, in the course of their observances, clergy of the different Churches, Armenian, Roman Catholic, Coptic and Orthodox jostle each other on the narrow street and at the Church of the Holy Sepulchre. The jostling between these Christians sometimes leads to fisticuffs as they celebrate significant events in the life of the Prince of Peace! In recent years fist fights between the clergy have led to the police being called and arrests being made. Another year some of the clergy ended up in hospital!

As we rambled slowly along the Via Dolorosa a large group of Christians from the subcontinent of India passed us with serious intent, chanting from small books on their way to the Church of the Holy Sepulchre. They looked like very ordinary people for whom this pilgrimage would probably be the high point of their lives and I marvelled at how devout they appeared and also how much it must have cost them to make the pilgrimage.

When we arrived at the Church of the Holy Sepulchre Eyal stayed at the edge of the forecourt, telling us that on pain of a huge fine he was not allowed to be our guide in the church. As we crossed the forecourt a man approached us, we assumed an official guide, offering to take us through the church. We declined on the grounds that we wanted to observe for ourselves and we did not want to be fed a line. The history of the church and of the site, going back to the first century, is complex and has been viewed over the centuries by people who are convinced of its authenticity and those who are not. At the end of the day, just like whether you believe there is a God at all or not, it is something, having taken account of the facts as you understand them, you either believe or you don't.

The first thing we saw inside the door on entering the church was a slab of stone on the ground with people kneeling all round it, praying, rubbing it with their hands and with handkerchiefs. One woman was rubbing it with a wad of cotton wool which she put into a small plastic bag. One or two people were leaning down and putting their cheeks on it. There were people standing waiting for a space to kneel and pushing in when one became available. This is believed to be the spot on which they placed Jesus when they took him down from the cross; the place where they anointed him before placing his body in the tomb. We wandered around the back to the tomb itself where, as it happened to be Whit Sunday, there was an Eastern Orthodox mass celebrated by a number of priests in elaborate red vestments. Some of them as they chanted were looking around at the tourists; they were fulfilling the form of the ritual and seemed to have only a tenuous involvement with what was going on at the centre. The whole building was an amazing complex of chapels, apses and walks. We walked around for a while observing the liturgies being performed in different chapels. There were tourists, like us, observing and there were devotees for whom being there was of serious religious import. There were a few women dressed entirely in black with black hoods, some sitting in corners perfectly still praying or meditating. One of them stood in front of a painting muttering a prayer, then reached up and ran her hand over as much of the picture as she could reach and made the sign of the cross repeatedly. On the way out a man encouraged us to go upstairs to the putative site of the crucifixion itself. We declined. We had had enough and left to rejoin Eyal.

Our next stop was the Tomb of David. Again Hilary had to go in the entrance to the women's section while Eyal and I went in the men's. The tomb is in a room of a former church. It consists of a stone sarcophagus covered with a blue cloth, that looks relatively new, on which there are Hebrew inscriptions. There are opposing views as to whether this is where David's body was placed after death or not. It is not even known whether the sarcophagus contains human remains. None the less it is an important place of pilgrimage, especially for Jews.

David is perhaps best known as the boy who killed the giant Goliath with a single stone from his catapult. He became God's anointed king of Israel and according to many biblical accounts in the books of First and Second Samuel he was, all in all, an unsavoury character. He is infamous for his affair with Bathsheba, wife of Uriah the Hittite an officer in his army. From his rooftop he saw Bathsheba in the distance in her bath and liked what he saw. He had her brought to him and ended up making her pregnant. He then connived to have Uriah make love to his wife so that he might think the child was his own, but failed. He ordered that Uriah be put in the front line of battle where he would more than likely be killed. He was. David is famous for his relationship with Jonathan of whom the Bible records that his love for Jonathan exceeded the love of women. Eyal referred to this and said that David was probably homosexual. I reminded him of the Bathsheba affair and suggested that it was far more likely that he was bisexual.

Needless to say that despite the evidence religious people will find a way around the difficulties of such biblical accounts and people who are anti-religious will espouse such stories. It is difficult to arrive at objective opinions about them.

We left the Tomb of David and Eyal was ready to show us more of Jerusalem but at this stage Hilary and I were exhausted. He smiled at our protestations, but readily agreed to return to the car. We arrived at the car park to find that he had overstayed his time and behind his windscreen wiper there was a ticket to pay a fine!

We had a good conversation with Eyal on the way back, mainly about immigration into Israel. After the fall of communism in Eastern Europe over one million Jews came to Israel, mainly from Russia. Having been used to bare shelves in the supermarkets back home, when they encountered the laden shelves in supermarkets in Israel there was a high instance of shoplifting. Israel is used to dealing with the problems of immigration and integration.

We were in good time on our return to *Gran Bretagna* and said goodbye to Eyal at the ramp. He had not pushed a line of any kind, religious or political. He had, I believe, answered our questions honestly. For example he said that he did not like the wall recently built along the West Bank, but it had reduced access of suicide bombers significantly and made much of Israel safer. Our visit had given us a lot to reflect upon.

Most people who think about it take one side or the other in the current Israeli/Palestinian conflict. I oscillate between the two, but with my sympathy more with the Palestinians. The Jews were in possession of the land in Old Testament times, when, thinking in the primitive religious terms of those days, they believed that God had given it to them and furthermore that they were God's chosen people, and we know what children think of teacher's pet. After the invasion of Judaea by the Babylonians in the sixth century BC and the destruction of the Temple many Jews were exiled from their homeland to Babylon in what was the beginning of the Jewish diaspora. A further impetus to this scattering occurred when the Romans destroyed the second Temple in 70 AD. The history of this talented, astute and able tribe of people for the next nearly 1,900 years is a story of the most appalling persecution, particularly by the Catholic Church. Luther hadn't much time for the Jews either. Persecution culminated in the holocaust of World War II, when 6 million Jews were killed in Nazi extermination camps. In 1947 the British, who occupied Palestine at the time, offered them a homeland there. This necessitated the displacement of Palestinians from land that their ancestors had occupied from forever. This of course is the root of the present conflict.

Before offering Palestine to the Jews, the British offered them a homeland in Uganda, which they turned down. This offer by the British of land that belonged to somebody else, the Ugandans, is hard to believe. It can only be understood in terms of the arrogant British imperial mentality of the time.

It is interesting to note that in 1934, for complex political reasons and needless to say all in the interests of Russian hegemony, the Soviet Union established a Jewish Autonomous Region for Soviet Jews in the Far East of Russia with Birobidzhan as its capital, to promote their own culture, with Yiddish as the language. In fact Jews were only ever a small minority in the region but even today, despite huge Jewish immigration into Israel from Russia after the fall of communism, there remains a small Jewish community in what is still called the Jewish Autonomous Region.

It is a complete nonsense to hold that God ever gave anybody land. Early people were on particular tracts of land for all kinds of reasons of chance and survival, but to say that God gave them land because they said so themselves and wrote it in their religious literature simply doesn't make sense. This is similar to the white South Africans justifying apartheid on the strength of a verse in the Old Testament. The Dutch Reformed Church of South Africa, to its credit, having supported this position for years finally affirmed some years before apartheid collapsed that such a claim was not justified. The devil quotes scripture for his purposes.

The image that the average lay person has of the Bible is that it is the word of God and because of this it is held in reverence. In other words that somehow God caused it to be written to tell the world what he wants to say to us. Many people think that the Bible is all of a piece in that it is consistent and if something is in the Bible it is thereby true. It is thought that if you want to know the right attitude to hold on some matter or the right thing to do in a human situation you will find it in the Bible. If you can quote scripture on an issue it gives you incontrovertible authority in the matter. Quite frankly this is nonsense.

The Bible is a collection of religious writings written over a period of about 1,500 years by a variety of authors in a variety of situations on religious topics of their time. Amongst the writings there are creation myths, history, poetry, liturgical texts, gospels and letters. It is fallacious to believe that any of these is the word of God. They are the opinion of the writers as to what they understood the word of God to be and some parts of the Bible contradict other parts. The writings reflect the religious thinking and beliefs of the writers and of their communities and it cannot be claimed that they are necessarily the thinking of God on any subject. They were given the authority which they have within the church as the word of God, inspired by God himself, because the church wanted to maintain authority for what it taught.

The Old Testament tells of a God who is a vengeful monster who says that he is a jealous god and his followers must kill anybody who doesn't believe in him. He encourages his followers to commit atrocities in his name. The New Testament is the response of the writers to Jesus, his life, death and resurrection.

The Bible is constantly misused by people to buttress their own opinions on many matters. For example homophobes use it to give authority to their condemnation of homosexuality. Amongst other texts, there are ten or twelve that condemn homosexuality; they quote the book of Leviticus that says that a man who lies with another man shall be put to death. Some verses later it says that a farmer who plants two different crops in his field or a woman who wears a garment made from two different materials shall be put to death. The last two verses are ignored while the verse condemning homosexuals is used by people who have taken it literally to justify their campaign against gays for no other reason than that they are gay. What does this say to us about the authority of the Bible? There is abroad an abysmal ignorance of this book. In a recent survey in America 35% of people polled believed that the Old Testament was written after Jesus' death, 10% believed that Joan of Arc was Noah's wife and a number thought that the epistles were the wives of the apostles. Another survey tells us that 45% of

Americans believe that the world was created according to the early books of Genesis and is less than 10,000 years old. The Bible contains a great deal of wisdom, helpful for people living in any age, but it also contains a lot of so called answers to our human condition that come from a time when the writers believed that God and heaven were somewhere up above the bright blue sky, we were here on a flat earth and the devil and hell were somewhere underground.

As we sailed out of Ashdod harbour into international waters in the small hours of the morning, we could not have known that in these same waters off Ashdod one week later the actions of Israeli armed forces would scandalise the world. Israeli troops killed 9 people when they boarded a ship of a flotilla from Turkey on its way to bring aid in the form of medical supplies and building materials to Gaza; yet another example of Israel's disproportionate use of force to terrorise Palestinians.

CHAPTER 6

At sea as a passenger on a cargo vessel your meals are put in front of you, your bed is made and your cabin is cleaned every morning, however you have to do your own washing and ironing. Passengers use the officers' washroom with washing machine, dryer, iron and ironing board. Hilary did the washing and drying and I did the ironing. This worked well until the washing machine broke down as it did shortly after we had left Ashdod. Now on a ship with a quota of marine engineers most things that fail to function can be made to work. In an engine room there is even a lathe which can be used to make parts, but it is doubtful if the cleverest marine engineer could make replacement parts for a washing machine, but employing sheer ingenuity I have no doubt that he could find a way around most problems. By evening the washing machine was working and clean clothes for passengers and crew were on the cards again.

The same day the Captain was in bad humour and it was nothing to do with the malfunctioning washing machine! He recounted to us that he had a recurring problem with his stomach. I have no doubt that the responsibilities and anxieties of a Captain at sea are considerable. I gave him a couple of Losec tablets from our medicine bag to try. Later when we met him he was all smiles; the Losec had worked a treat.

We sailed past the southwest coast of Crete en route to the Strait of Messina on our way to the next port of call, Salerno for the second time. On the way south from Salerno on the outward journey we had passed through the Strait of Messina in the middle of the night in rough weather. Now on the way back we passed through them midday and in beautiful weather. On this leg of the voyage, we had some wonderful blue skies, sparkling sea and it was warm, very warm. We sat on deck in the Mediterranean sun to relax, to read, and away from the everyday concerns of life ashore, to reflect and to ruminate like Sean O'Casey's Joxer: 'What is the stars?' The answers that the Christian communities of Jerusalem gave to the great questions of life were to the forefront of my mind. There are no answers to all the big questions about religion and most people don't want to think about them. Those that do often give religious answers that come solely from their indoctrination; they come from the heart and take no account of the head. Chekhov described these answers as 'absurd nonsense.'

Some hours after we had passed through the Strait, we could see on our starboard side a small conically shaped island shrouded in mist. I asked the officer on watch what it was. 'Stromboli' he replied. There are names buried deep in our memories from childhood, often with associations we have long forgotten. 'Stromboli' was for me one of those names. All I remembered was that it was a volcano, and I assumed that the memory was from school. It may have become lodged in my mind because of the sound of the name. It is a name that a child would make up. I took some photographs, but the mist allowed me to capture only a fuzzy outline. I would look up 'Stromboli' when I came home.

Stromboli is one of a ring of eight small islands in the Tyrrhenian Sea north of Sicily. It is a continuously mildly active volcano, characterised by internal explosive activity that only rarely leads to lava flow. The biggest eruption in recent times was in 1930 when several people were killed and some buildings were destroyed. In 2002 a larger than usual eruption caused the island to close to non-residents. Three or four hundred people live in two villages at the foot of the volcano. The larger of the villages has some hotels to cater for a small tourist trade. The island was the location of an eponymous film starring Ingrid Bergman made in 1950, written and directed by Roberto Rossellini. It is perfectly possible that this is why the name lodged in my memory.

We expected to be in Salerno by 18.00 hours, but didn't dock until 22.00. With our experience of eating there last time we had planned to have a meal in Amalfi, but these plans were dashed. It was too late to go ashore. The good news, however, was that next day we would have time to spend most of the day at Pompeii where neither of us had been before. I knew that Pompeii was a Roman town that had been destroyed by the eruption of Vesuvius and had been excavated in modern times. I knew little else.

We took a taxi from the ramp to the railway station in Salerno to catch an 8.30am train to Pompeii. The taxi driver confounded my opinion of his tribe, though I have always conceded that exceptions do exist. He brought us into the station to show us the ticket office and then left. We were just arriving upstairs at the platform when he appeared again to ensure that we were at the right platform; a man concerned to be helpful to visitors or, betraying my prejudice against taxi drivers, a ruse in the hope of getting another tip! A twenty five or thirty minute train journey, a short taxi ride and we were at the main entrance.

Pompeii is at the foot of the volcano Vesuvius on the rim of the Bay of Naples. It was a thriving Roman city of 20,000 inhabitants when in 62 AD a violent earthquake shook the region causing Pompeii extensive damage. Reconstruction was still in progress when on 24th August 79 AD suddenly Vesuvius, for centuries considered extinct, erupted and buried the town under ash and rock. The author Pliny the Younger who lived at Misenum across the Bay with his uncle, Pliny the Elder, has left an eye witness account of the catastrophe.

'Flames from the volcano soared high into the sky and an immense black cloud soon rose above them blacking out the sun. Volcanic matter, lapilli and red hot scoriae, rained down on Pompeii, walls and roofs crumbled, then ashes mixed with water fell until all forms of life were extinguished. Darkness reigned and the scene was made even more apocalyptic by lightning, earthquakes and tidal waves. The few survivors who sought to escape were overtaken and killed by the poison gasses which spread everywhere. The inferno continued for three days and then all was silence. A layer of death, from 15 to 20 feet deep covered the area.'

Pliny the Elder, also an author, sailed across the bay, some say to observe the eruption at close quarters; he was a naturalist. Others say he went to rescue friends. He arrived, but died on the shore, perhaps of fumes or maybe of natural causes.

For 1,800 years Pompeii lay largely undisturbed. There was a superstitious fear of the site. In the mid 18th century some excavation was begun under the King of Naples, but it was 1858 before excavation began in earnest. As work progressed the archaeologist in charge devised a way of pouring plaster of Paris into the spaces left by decomposed organic matter. By this method, the forms of human bodies, animals and even some plants were preserved. Three quarters of the city has been excavated, and work on the remaining quarter continues. The layout and walls of streets of houses, shops, and other buildings survive. Streets, with primitive street lighting; fragments of quartz set between the paving stones to reflect light on moonlit nights, footpaths and public areas are preserved. A theatre and one of the finest Roman amphitheatres in the world have survived in relatively good condition. There are temples to different gods, Apollo, Venus, Jupiter, public baths, a sports field, brothels, municipal offices. There is art, some religious, some erotic, in the form of frescos, some in amazing states of conservation, and sculpture.

One visitors' handbook says that all the important public news of the city was written on the walls of public buildings by scriptores. On the walls also are many notes from shopkeepers, lovers, students, sports fans, tourists and even swindlers and procurers. With these graffiti people of that time talk to us about the concerns of their daily lives of 2000 years ago.

Everything in this Roman city reflects the same human activities that exist in any city of today. *Plus ça change....* Essential human wants and needs and necessities are constant in every age across the universal range of cultures and of peoples. Pompeii is a wondrous work of excavation and conservation and it would take weeks or even months to do it justice.

After three or four hours walking in the hot sun, we were exhausted. Rubbernecking is a tiring business, especially when you are no longer 21. We left by the gate beside the amphitheatre and found 'Ristorante Amfiteatro' nearby. We sat outside under a rustic framework covered with an ancient wisteria. We were the only ones there and we rested our weary feet. We were having a wonderful garlic and herb spaghetti, the likes of which you can only get in Italy, when the place was invaded by a busload of Americans with not a word to say for themselves! This in no way interfered with our delightful lunch. We did some people-watching and were amused by the diversity of people that ended up on a tour bus together.

We walked to the station, got a train to Salerno, a taxi to the ship and rested our weary bodies before going on deck to watch the loading of even more cars.

We left Salerno for the second time; our course set north west for Savona, a small port on the Gulf of Genoa. On board were a new Captain and a new cook, the two most important men on the ship. When we were set fair I went to the Captain's cabin and knocked on the door.

'Come in.' He was sitting at his desk and stood up immediately I entered. He smiled and shook hands.

'I've come to ask your permission to go onto the bridge.'

'Yes, he said, I have no difficulty at all. If a problem …..' and I anticipated him:

'We will leave.'

'No need,' he said, 'just stand to one side.' I thanked him and left. That was the one and only time we spoke for the rest of the trip. When we met he would smile and say 'buongiorno' or 'buonasera' but he did not make conversation like his predecessor. It seemed strange to us that he didn't ask us where we were from, where we had joined the ship or whether we were enjoying the trip. It seemed to us that as a generalisation the Filipinos had much better inter-personal skills than the Italians. They asked us questions and we had good interactive conversations with them. They were however more competent in English.

This Captain was a big man; six feet three or four inches tall but less well proportioned than the first Captain. For the whole length of his tall frame he was broad. He had a soft oblong face with pendulous double chin. He was amply, but uniformly, covered and walked with the waddle of the obese. He interacted with the other officers in much the same way as the last Captain had, sometimes holding court on the bridge with junior officers who listened intently to him and laughed from time to time. He may have been genuinely humorous or it might have been diplomatic for the young officers to listen to him. Not understanding Italian we could not tell. I commented to one of the officers:

'This Captain doesn't spend as much time on the bridge as the last one.'

'No. He's in his cabin watching TV.'

One morning when we went down to breakfast, the Captain was sitting by himself at the junior officers' table dunking his bread roll in his coffee watching cartoons on television. There was a better view of the TV from the junior officers' table than from the Captain's table.

The new cook, Andrea, was a particularly pleasant man in his early forties. According to one of the officers he was a better cook than Lanzo, his predecessor, had been. We saw little difference between them.

We sailed north west, off the coast of Italy and passed close to the island of Elba, between it and the north east coast of Corsica. It was, of course, the first place of exile of Napoleon and well known for the palindrome: 'Able was I ere I saw Elba.' I hadn't ever thought where Elba was, or how the Little Corporal managed to escape, but I now realised that it was close to his homeland of Corsica which perhaps facilitated his plans. If he had been exiled to St. Helena in the South Atlantic in the first place, the 'hundred days' would not have been. There would have been no need for the Battle of Waterloo, which would have saved the Duke of Wellington a lot of trouble, the language would have been deprived of one of its well known metaphors about a person coming to grief, and they would have had to find another name for the London railway station.

We saw a lot of dolphins in the Ligurian Sea between Corsica and Savona. I thought all along that the dolphins we had seen were young ones, but now realised that looking down to the sea from the height we were at on the bridge, adult dolphins just looked small.

Savona is on the Italian Riviera west of Genoa. Christopher Columbus farmed land outside Savona in his early days and Savona claims that it is the place of his birth. He had lived there as a youth, but that he was born there is unsubstantiated. It is more likely that he was born along the coast in Genoa. The other famous resident of the area was Guilliano Della Rovere who became Pope Julius II, the Warrior Pope, who was said to have been happier armour-clad leading his troops into battle than vestment-clad leading worship in the Vatican. He did, however, have one notable achievement; in the year 1505 he put in train the building of the present St Peter's Basilica that took 120 years to complete.

We docked close enough for us to have only a short walk through the old harbour to the town. The main streets of the town were typically Italian of the 18th and 19th centuries; colonnades on both sides with beautifully frescoed ceilings and as it was Saturday, market day, there were stalls under the colonnades selling fruit, cheese, vegetables, bread, oil and much else. There were stalls too down side streets. Here and there along the streetscape of more recent buildings there was the façade of a Rococo Church or some other ancient building.

We had plenty of time in hand and strolled back to the delightful old harbour. There were fishermen on their boats mending nets and talking across to each other. On the quay there were men gutting fish straight from the boats and selling them to discerning housewives. We sat in the sun and watched. There was an old fashioned atmosphere and pace about what we saw. Although our Italian wasn't up to knowing what people were talking about, we could see that their conversation was relaxed, humorous and good humoured.

We walked back to the ship and went out onto the top deck. It was hot, humid and still. There were no other ships. *Gran Bretagna* had finished discharging. We looked down from the stern on the quay side. Jesus, the AB on duty, strolled over and back at the top of the ramp. George, the second officer appeared. In ten minutes time there were four crew members walking around kicking their heels. They disappeared into the ship and shortly afterwards Jesus returned. Then George appeared again. After about ten minutes two taxis came along the dock and stopped at the foot of the ramp. The drivers stayed in their cars. They sat there for a few minutes and then one driver got out and walked up the ramp, talked to George who made a phone call and went back to the taxi man. He returned to the taxis and talked to the other driver. One taxi went further up the dock and disappeared and the other turned around and returned to the town. Nothing happened for another ten minutes or so. George had gone and Jesus sat on the rail smoking a cigarette. Then a man on an autocycle arrived, stopped at the end of the ramp, took a reflective jacket and briefcase from under his saddle, donned the jacket, walked up the ramp and disappeared into the ship. Ten minutes later he reappeared, put the jacket and briefcase under his saddle, started the motor and put, put, putted back towards the town. Nothing for a few minutes and then a deck boy appeared on the deck below us, looked down on the empty ramp and disappeared. Then the sound of a motor warming up. The winch turned, the steel hawsers tightened and the ramp was lifted slowly off the quay. It took six or seven minutes for it to lift into place. Ropes from the ship were still secured to bollards. The quay was deserted and the heat and humidity were palpable. After a few minutes from nowhere a little man appeared. The ropes at the stern were slackened from the ship, the little man took them off the bollards and dropped them into the water and they were hauled aboard. I looked towards the bow and there was another man freeing ropes from the bollards there. The Captain and pilot were at the control console on the wing of the bridge. The ship moved a few feet out from the quay and then went forward. We moved slowly toward the harbour mouth and out into the bay. We were on our way south to the Strait of Gibraltar and from there north to the Portuguese port of Setubal. It would take two and a half days.

At sea, since Limassol, I was re-reading Joyce's *Portrait of an Artist*. Leaving Savona I had come to the passage that led to one of its best known quotations: 'Ireland is the old sow that eats her farrow.'

When the soul of man is born in this country there are nets flung at it to hold it back from flight. You talk to me of nationality, language, religion. I shall try to fly by those nets.

Davin knocked the ashes from his pipe.

Too deep for me, Stevie, he said. But a man's country comes first. Ireland first, Stevie. You can be a poet or mystic after.

Do you know what Ireland is? asked Steven with cold violence. Ireland is the old sow that eats her farrow.'

All my life I have had a sense of wanting to 'fly by those nets,' to avoid the constraints of nationality, language and religion. My family came to Ireland in the early nineteenth century from England, but originally from Scotland. My paternal grandfather who died in 1909 was in the army in Ireland and in India. His brother was a surgeon in the Indian Army. In 1885 my grandfather was a member of the famous Nile Expedition that was sent to rescue General Gordon in Khartoum. After the expedition failed he was posted back to Ireland and ended up as a recruitment officer at the barracks in Wexford where he died. My father was born in Wexford and I was born there thirty years after my grandfather's death. That's how I came to be from Wexford. My maternal grandfather served in the RIC in Cork from where my mother came. Both my parents, who were adult in 1922, as citizens gave the new state their full, but not uncritical, loyalty.

Since I was a boy, born and brought up in the south of Ireland, I have always wanted to free myself from the narrow, self-conscious and extravagant national pride that was all around me. I was born only seventeen years after independence so as I grew up I heard at every turn the espousal of Ireland and everything Irish but always felt that self praise is no praise. I became aware that this narrow and extravagant Irish Nationalism came from a national inferiority complex that resulted from having been a colonised people, and particularly a colonised people on the doorstep of the coloniser. Some teachers and I understand especially Christian Brothers, indoctrinated young children with a nationalism that sometimes amounted to hatred of Britain and then we wonder why violent republicanism still rears its ugly head. If you sow the wind you reap the whirlwind.

I once heard a language enthusiast on radio say that unless you speak Irish you're not a proper Irishman. According to this principle I am numbered among the ninety five percent or more defective Irish people who, although they may have a nodding acquaintance with school Irish, certainly don't speak the language. I have always, however, been in favour of preserving the spoken language as far as possible. I marvel at the naïveté of Irish governments that believed the making of Irish compulsory in schools would result in due course in the general use of the language in everyday life. I think it is clear now that compulsion over the years rather than increase the use of Irish probably contributed to its diminution. Two different native speaker friends who love their first language and use it when they can, independently have told me that sometimes so bad is the Irish that they hear spoken on radio and television they cannot bear to listen to it and they turn it off.

Having been brought up a member of the Church of Ireland in the post independence period of triumphalist Catholicism, there is a sense in which I was made to feel an outsider. For so many people, both in Ireland and outside, Irish is synonymous with Roman Catholic. However Brendan Corish, the leader of the Labour party in the 1960s, went even further and, contrary to Davin's belief, said publicly: 'I am a Catholic first and an Irishman second.' I resented being seen by fellow countrymen as being Irish but not the full shilling. I also resented that being Irish, foreigners expected me to sit lightly to the law and to have an ongoing affair with alcohol.

How then am I Irish?

I am Irish pure and simple. I am as Irish as the most extreme republican, as the greatest enthusiast for and most fluent speaker of the Irish language and as the most fervent Roman Catholic. I am neither proud nor ashamed of it. It was an accident of birth. I am glad that I am Irish and I know that I could never live contentedly outside Ireland. There are characteristics of Irish people that I appreciate: generosity to the afflicted, welcome to the stranger, a relaxed approach to living and a particular sense of humour. However none of these is exclusive to our people; they are all present to varying degrees in the character of the people of other nations. We are not God's gift to the world. We are one of a multitude of peoples on the planet who happen to live together within particular national boundaries. There are characteristics of many Irish people that I do not appreciate, for example the selfishness of being so laid back as to be unreliable and believing that the destructive use of alcohol is funny. These two, of course, are not exclusive to us either.

I'm not a Kerry Republican, a Dublin 4 Nationalist nor an Ulster or any other kind of Unionist. I'm not a Gaeilgeóir or a Roman Catholic. On the other hand I am not Anglo Irish in any sense; I don't possess, nor ever did possess a horse! Nor have I an emotional home in England or elsewhere for that matter. There are characteristics of English people and people of other nationalities that I appreciate, but I don't want to be other than Irish. I am simply a human being that happens to have been born on the island of Ireland, and I'm glad that I was.

From Hilary's notes I see that on the day that we left Savona, for lunch we had: spaghetti with oil, picante and tomato, followed by a plate of grilled courgette slices with raw garlic and chilli flakes and a banana. For dinner: soup with lentils, pizza, cheese and strawberries and melon in syrup. Across from us the junior officer carnivores had thick slices of beef.

Again we had good warm sunny weather on this part of the voyage. We sailed offshore, but well to sea and out of sight of the coast of Italy, France and Spain. The chart on the bridge told us that we passed well known places: Monaco, Nice, Cannes, Toulon,

Barcelona and then between Majorca and Ibiza and the Spanish coast.

At this point there was a message on the telex, similar to the one we received between Ithica and Crotone about a missing lone yachtsman. This time we were asked to keep an eye out for a white catamaran with three people, two adults and a child, that was overdue between Minorca and Sardinia. However the area mentioned was way east of our course.

We passed Valencia, Alicante and then places familiar to sun and sand holiday makers: Malaga, Torremolinos, Fuengirola and Marbella. Passing along this coast we could see the snow capped peaks of the Sierra Nevada. Since we left Savona we had seen more dolphins than we had seen on the rest of the voyage. Sometimes they seemed to play chicken as they surfaced and then dived close to the bow of the ship.

Gibraltar is not, as I always thought, the southernmost tip of land attached to the end of Spain facing North Africa. It is the end of a small peninsula to the east of the southernmost tip of Spain. It was ceded to Britain in 1713 at the settlement after the War of the Spanish Succession. It has been British ever since and likely to remain so. Periodically Spain claims it back and Britain's policy is that it will stay British as long as the Gibraltarians want it so, in this respect the same as Britain's policy towards the six counties of Northern Ireland. In 1967 a referendum on the issue was held and 99 per cent of residents of Gibraltar voted to stay with Britain.

The Irish association? Gibraltar was the childhood place of Molly Bloom:

'All the way from Gibraltar. Forgotten any little Spanish she knew,'

from where her bedstead came, bought by her father:

'Wonder what her father gave for it. Old style. Ah yes, of course. Bought it at the governor's auction.'

In 1988 in Gibraltar there was a controversial killing of three members of an IRA active service unit. They had plans to plant a bomb to kill members of a British military band at the governor's residence. The three should have been arrested rather than shot.

In recent times there have been two major shipping tragedies off Europa Point, the very tip of Gibraltar. In August 2007 *New Flame*, a Panamanian registered bulk carrier, collided with a Danish oil tanker and ended up half submerged on a reef. All the crew were rescued. The ship eventually broke in two and sank. In October 2008 *Fedra*, another bulk carrier, registered in Liberia, in severe gale force 12 winds ran aground on Europa Point itself. All the crew were rescued and this ship also broke in two. In contrast *Gran Bretagna* had fine calm weather on 31st May when we left the Rock, one of Europe's best known landmarks and with Europa Point on our starboard side passed through the Strait on course for Setubal.

One of the great things about being a passenger on a cargo ship is that you have no responsibilities and this gives you plenty of time to reflect. You have time to mull over questions that you had as an idealistic youth, questions that have dogged you all of your life and thoughts that you have from the perspective of advancing years. Gibraltar was given to Britain at a time when Europe was ruled by emperors and kings who believed that they governed by divine right, that is, with direct authority from God. They made alliances and fought each other to defend or extend their kingdoms. They particularly fought when one of them died and the succession to a throne was not clear-cut and succession one way or the other would upset the balance of power in Europe. So intermarried were the royal families of Europe that when there was not an obvious heir to a vacant throne, there were plenty of hopeful royals from other countries who considered they had a chance of claiming it and were prepared to go to war to do so. These royal families were never satisfied with what they had, but wanted more. They were prepared to sacrifice the lives of thousands and sometimes hundreds of thousands of troops to satisfy their own egos and their own greed. They were like the bankers and developers of recent times in our own country who never had enough and in pursuit of their own egos and greed destroyed our economy and left hundreds of thousands of ordinary citizens in dire straits. The emperors and kings never had enough and when hundreds of thousands of their subjects had been slaughtered in battle they would eventually sit down and share out the spoils of war.

After one such war, the War of the Spanish Succession, when the chief contenders for the Spanish throne, the Hapsburgs and the Bourbons each supported by other royal houses of Europe, shared out the spoils like schoolboys sharing out apples after they had robbed an orchard, two pieces of land, Gibraltar and Minorca, were ceded to Britain.

Most often the problems created by the occupation of land are best understood as tribal. We think of tribalism as something confined to primitive societies, for example in countries of Africa or South America. How these countries work cannot be understood unless you understand the tribal dynamic within them, and tribes often extend across the modern state borders of two or more countries, creating a further complication. Tribes have religious rituals that are distinctive to themselves that their tribal priests perform at their own tribal shrine. Language and religion are inextricably bound together with tribal identity. Now apply this to tribalism in so called civilised countries, for example: Ireland; Nationalist and Unionist. Palestine; Israeli and Arab. Belgium; Flemish and Walloon, Cyprus; Turkish and Greek, Gibraltar; Spanish and British and almost any country where in history there has been occupation by another country. None of these problems is any the less tribal than problems in what citizens of these countries would consider less civilised societies of the world, but tribal they are. With tribalism synonymous with nationalism, we are back to Joyce's 'nationalism, language and religion.'

In the past politicians were masters at exploiting these issues of tribe, language and religion for their own ends. They exploited them to be and stay elected and to acquire and stay in power. Many still do this, but today this is seen for what it is; the shameless reinforcing of divisions amongst peoples which is not so acceptable these days, and politicians in some countries are embarrassed to be so openly divisive.

We can easily make the mistake of believing that politicians are ordinary human beings that think and act in the same ways as the rest of us. They aren't. Many politicians on the face of it are decent people, but you ought to deal with them on the assumption that the most important thing in their lives is to secure votes to get them elected next time out. They will say and do anything to that end and being pleasant, sociable, decent, honest or anything else will be secondary to that. Now that I have got all that off my chest, where were we? Leaving the Mediterranean and sailing into the Atlantic on our way to Setubal.

CHAPTER 7

We had been hoping that having docked in Setubal we would have enough time ashore to get to Lisbon; this turned out not to be the case. My interest in Lisbon is the earthquake of 1755. It happened in the morning of 1st November, All Saints' Day at approximately 9.40 am when, it being a Church festival, most of the population were on their way to, or were already in, church. It is estimated that the quake lasted over three minutes and brought down a large portion of the city's buildings, including churches where thousands of worshippers were killed. The quake caused the sea to recede completely from the coast so that witnesses recounted having seen lost cargo and shipwrecks lying on the sea-bed. Then the ocean returned in the form of a tsunami in which thousands of the survivors of the quake were drowned. More people who survived the quake and tsunami were killed in the fire that lasted for three days. It is estimated that between quake, tsunami and fire 85 per cent of the city was destroyed and as many as 60,000 people were killed. Shocks from the earthquake were felt as far away as Finland, North Africa and Galway where it caused damage to the Spanish Arch.

At that time it was one of the worst earthquakes in history and resulted in the beginnings of the modern science of seismology. Needless to say there was speculation amongst theologians and philosophers as to God's involvement in the matter. It caused Voltaire to revise his support for the philosopher Leibnitz's view that we live in the best of all possible worlds. Subsequently he satirised this view in his novel 'Candide'.

Setubal (pronounced Stubal) is the third largest city of Portugal after Lisbon and Oporto. It is only 25 miles from Lisbon and it is inevitable that it suffered massive destruction in the 1755 earthquake. It was a warm, sunny early June day when we walked the short distance from the dock to the town. The centre of this old port is enchanting. The little streets and squares are paved with flat cobbles in mosaic patterns. The footpaths of larger streets are similarly paved. This is the distinctively Portuguese feature we saw for the first time in the Azores when we landed there at the unscheduled end of our previous cargo ship voyage. One of Setubal's main streets was lined with trees in a profusion of pink blossom. We sat outside a cafe in a square and watched a large assembly of schoolchildren with their teachers publicising care for the environment. We had lunch in the sun outside another café where we had difficulty in making ourselves understood. While we have only a little Italian, needless to say we haven't a word of Portuguese. As in Salerno we did hit on one Portuguese word: 'omelete,' spelled with one 't,' and simultaneously pointing to some cheese and to chips on the plate of another diner ordered a satisfactory lunch. For football fans: Setubal is the home town of José Mourinho. For non-football fans; he is manager of Real Madrid, a quite well-known Spanish football team. He is famous internationally and considered one of the best managers in the world of football.

We strolled back to the ship and in the evening set sail on the last leg of our voyage to Portbury, the port of Bristol. The weather was good so we had no repeat of turbulence of sea or stomach as we passed by the Bay of Biscay. We sailed close to Land's End and past Lundy Island into the Bristol Channel. We docked in Portbury in the early morning of the third day out of Setubal. We left *Gran Bretagna* and took a taxi into Bristol. Naturally the taxi driver spoke English; he was retired and drove a taxi for occupation and to augment his pension and I am certain did not pull any taxi driver stunts on us. He delivered us to the home of Lewis, a cousin of mine, and Joan his wife with whom we were to stay at the end of our four week voyage. You will remember that on the night before we sailed from Southampton we stayed with another cousin in Winchester. I have my grandparents to thank for having cousins in many convenient places.

AFTERWORD

Thus ended a second successful voyage on which Hilary and I met interesting people, passengers and crew, and we visited interesting places. We found these voyages exciting and were at one as to how to spend our time on board and ashore. Aboard we sat in the sun and read and spent time on the bridge reading co-ordinates to follow our route. We simply enjoyed being at sea despite its humours. We learned the ways of mariners as they went about their work, and we relished the anticipation of going ashore at the next port of call. We have carried with us precious memories of sea, sky, mariners and the pleasure of many foreign places.

I leave the last word to Hilary:

'Having lived for many years beside the sea, it was a thrill to live on it for weeks at a time. There was the reassuring throb of the engine and the constant pattern of the wake. To experience at night the vista of sea meeting the starlit canopy of sky filled me with wonder. Thoughts of sea travellers through the ages traversing these same waters and seeing these same stars, left a deep and lasting impression on me of the transitory nature of living.'

About the Author

Patrick Semple is a former Church of Ireland clergyman. Patrick has had two volumes of memoirs published, and two collections of poems. He was editor of 'A Parish Adult Education Handbook,' and ghost wrote 'That Could Never Be,' a memoir by Kevin Dalton. He has had short stories published and broadcast. His novel 'Transient Beings' was published in 2012.

Patrick teaches a creative writing course at the National University of Ireland Maynooth, Adult Education Department and for the last three years has done public readings of his work in Kempten, Bavaria.

He has a website at *www.patricksemple.ie*

TRANSIENT BEINGS
A novel by Patrick Semple

Some transient beings come from the past and pass through the present and some in the present refuse to leave the past. How long will the idyllic rectory in the heart of rural Ireland in the 1970's hide the secrets of those who live behind its walls?

Patrick Semple's writing has been described as having a depth of learning and an earnestness of purpose with a selfless immersion in the lives of the characters in the best traditions of John McGahern and Brian Moore.

Transient Beings is a surprising, intelligent and brave story of addiction and belief. It is also the story of the rector as he struggles to understand his duty, his wife and his place in the world. It is a story from the heart as we follow the rector into a growing nightmare of rationalisation. It gives a voice to those people whose life is religion and who find they are forced to reassess their own beliefs.

'There is no greater heresy than that the office sanctifies the holder of it.' and this is as true for the rector's wife as it is for the rector.

Lightning Source UK Ltd.
Milton Keynes UK
UKOW042247200313

207952UK00001B/3/P